LITTLE BOOK OF

ROLEX

Published in 2024 by Welbeck
An imprint of the Welbeck Publishing Group
Offices in: London – 20 Mortimer Street, London W1T 3JW &
Sydney – Level 17, 207 Kent St, Sydney NSW 2000 Australia
www.welbeckpublishing.com

Design and layout © Welbeck Non-Fiction Limited 2024
Text © Josh Sims 2024

A CIP catalogue for this book is available from the British Library.

ISBN 978-1-80279-759-6

Printed in China

10 9 8 7 6 5 4 3 2 1

LITTLE BOOK OF

ROLEX

The story of the iconic brand

JOSH SIMS

WELBECK

CONTENTS

INTRODUCING
ROLEX

YOU NEED HANS

The story goes that Hans Wilsdorf was sitting on a London double-decker bus when the name for his fledgling watch company came to him.

I t was pronounceable for a speaker of any language; it was punchy, memorable and short, so would fit easily on any dial; and, he imagined, it echoed the sound of a mechanical watch being wound. Rolex would go on to become not just the biggest watch brand in the world in terms of name recognition but also one of the top five brands in the world full stop. Remarkable for a product that only the few rather than the many get to own. Ask someone with no interest in watches to name a watch company, ask them anywhere in the world, and they will almost certainly say: "Rolex".

Yet Rolex is an enigma – even as it's globally known, thanks to its sponsorship of high-profile sporting events, its resonance in film and pop culture and the fact that its designs are, arguably,

OPPOSITE Rolex isn't just the world's biggest watch brand but one of the world's biggest of all brands, known the globe over.

the most widely copied in all watchmaking history. Its watches are not notably expensive – relative to the watches of many other historic makers at least – nor does it make only a few. The Geneva-based company is reputed to make around 800,000 pieces every year – more than other watchmakers produce in their entire histories. But Rolex does not discuss figures, or talk about all it does. "We don't feel the need," said chairman Bertrand Gros enigmatically in 2014.

And that's true of so much else: Rolex rarely discusses anything about what it does. It is a private company in every sense of the word, owned by a non-profit trust and so not subject to the requirements of financial disclosure faced by publicly traded companies. It shares the culture of Swiss banking – opaque, distanced, impenetrable unless it sees advantage. Rolex operates out of what it calls its administrative "mega-blocks". In Geneva, it combines offices and factory in a monolith designed by Addor, Juilliard & Bolliger; the gridded glass box headquarters were later transformed by brodbeck roulet, all those reflective surfaces seeming to bounce back any outside enquiries. In Lausanne, the Rolex Learning Centre, a "laboratory for learning", is 20,000 square metres (215,000 square feet) of a single continuous undulation in profile, looking from the sky like nothing less than a huge main plate from the innards of one of its watches.

This is architecture that is eye-catching and yet also restrained. Much like Rolex, which rarely launches a new model that deviates radically from anything it was doing back in the 1960s or before. Even so, the brand can lay claim to having several stand-out and eminently wearable classics in its portfolio, each seemingly unisex in their appeal and each still in production – icons not just among watches but icons of design more broadly. Other watchmakers strive for decades to have maybe one.

That also means that on the outside its watches are all so

familiar, at least superficially – thanks in part to the way its original designs have inspired so many cheaper imitations, and in part to the way their tireless cachet has seen them endlessly counterfeited. Rolex fanatics will say that it's all in the tiniest of details, with even the placement or colour of the typography on a Rolex dial able to give rise to a huge premium on the secondary market.

And yet the company has also pioneered airtightness, dustproofing, waterproofing and, latterly, materials science and the development of new alloys to improve the hardy functionality of its timepieces – all in-house, all the better to protect those precious, patented ideas. Since the 1990s Rolex has been almost entirely vertically integrated: if it does anything, it does it itself.

Many may aspire to own a Rolex – both watch fans, who may consider at least one Rolex to be an essential part of any collection, and those who want just one quality watch for life, who see a Rolex as the definitive watch. A Rolex has become the go-to spend for life's benchmarks – a generous gift to mark a 21st birthday, or a gift to oneself to mark a first bonus. Few things quietly announce having "arrived" – for men and women alike – as a Rolex. The company could undoubtedly sell many, many more pieces than it makes.

RIGHT One of the earliest Rolex Oyster watches, before its Perpetual automatic movement, and marked "Precision" even before gaining COSC certification.

And yet, all the better to maintain that desirability, its new models are, notoriously, very hard to acquire – like other luxury goods companies, it seems to operate an unofficial system by which long-time, loyal customers of its lesser models are finally invited to buy one of its more rarefied ones. And everyone else can wait. Or buy at a premium at auction. Or, most likely, just look on dreamily.

Rolex is, then, a mass of intriguing, beguiling contradictions. It's an industrial maker of mostly simple, *form follows function*, stainless steel watches that some say are overpriced and under-specced. And it's true, Rolex is not the maker of the best watches in the world, if judged by technical complexity. It's also the brand that is said to invest almost a third of its revenue in marketing – one of the conditions of Wilsdorf insisting the company be run as a foundation – somewhat suggesting a situation of style over substance, cool over content. What's more a Rolex watch – through no fault of the company – came to symbolize a kind of vulgarity, a flashiness, a lack of imagination on the part of the consumer…

And yet, and yet… At the same time this is Rolex, transcending the naysayers, and so much bigger than all that. Certainly it is a testament to Rolex that despite these doubts, despite the seeming ubiquity of its products, the watches it makes are still so in demand, so much still a talisman of success. There is the aura of Oz around Rolex – the magic, the mythology and the mystique – though with this Oz the curtain is never pulled back to reveal the wizard.

Rolex really does generate a passion among its devotees that few other watch brands can claim. New model variations quickly acquire their own nicknames, be that a green bezelled "Hulk" or the "Smurf" with its bright blue dial. Small wonder, then, that the love of Rolex has been described as being something akin to a cult. It is not hard to understand why.

TIME
TRAVELLERS

A BRIEF HISTORY OF ROLEX

Hans Wilsdorf's introduction to the world of watches
came at the age of 19.

Having attended boarding school and then business school, Wilsdorf travelled from his native Bavaria, now part of Germany, to La Chaux-de-Fonds, the epicentre of Swiss watchmaking, getting a job with a pearl dealer and then with Cuno Korten, an exporter of Swiss pocket watches. One of his jobs each day was to wind up several hundred of these in order to monitor their accuracy. The environs of his work perhaps only reassured him that the watch industry did not understand what modern customers needed – timepieces that were less fancy and more functional, more rational and, in some sense, more Germanic – and that this was a gap he could fill.

OPPOSITE A defining characteristic of Rolex – as on this Daytona – is the winding crown signed with the brand's iconic five-point crown logo.

"My work there provided an excellent opportunity to study the watchmaking industry closely and to examine every type of watch produced both in Switzerland and abroad," Wilsdorf noted in *Rolex Jubilee Vade Mecum*, a small book that he wrote himself in 1946.

In 1905, aged 24 and after completing his National Service back in Bavaria, Wilsdorf moved to London and became a British citizen. He borrowed some money from his mother and sister and, with his English brother-in-law, Alfred Davis, established Wilsdorf & Davis on London's jewellery street, Hatton Garden, as an importer and distributor of Swiss watches. Davis was largely a silent partner, but Wilsdorf had big plans, with the intention for them to produce their own watch. This would be something simple and robust but handsome enough to be worn on the wrist, in line with a growing fashion, rather than hidden away in a pocket, as watches typically had been. The name for Wilsdorf's new brand, Rolex, came to him while on a horse-drawn omnibus through London in 1908. He is said to have come up with over 100 possible names before settling on Rolex.

A NEW ERA

The naming of the company in this way was bold enough: until then a pocket watch almost exclusively carried the family names of its maker on the dial, suggesting as it did tradition, craft, provenance. In fact, it proved hard for Wilsdorf to find acceptance for this approach, such that he started out putting the Rolex name on just one in six of its watches, only slowly adding it to more. That would prove to be just the first of Rolex's many innovations. In 1925, to get the Rolex name known, Wilsdorf not only created the brand's five-point crown logo, but decided to spend what was then a small fortune on advertising.

This paid off, with dealers gradually accepting that having "Rolex" on the dials of its watches was a sales benefit rather than a hindrance. The Art Deco-inspired Rolex Prince of 1928 was a major hit and helped establish Rolex as a serious name in watchmaking.

But Wilsdorf would be a fount of innovation. From the outset, he said, he also wanted to create no-nonsense watch designs, which is one reason why no Rolex has ever had a crystal caseback in order to view the movement – that would just make the movement less well-protected. He wanted watches that were suitable for both men and women too, essentially unisex bar some changes to sizing. This was another radical idea for the

ABOVE Before the Oyster case or the Perpetual movement, Rolex focused on making watches in fashionable designs, but always pitching accuracy as its standout quality.

If you were racing here tomorrow

you'd wear a Rolex.

Sliding through this right-angle bend a Formula One Grand Prix car is travelling roughly 8 yards in a fifth of a second.

So to say Grand Prix racing drivers have a highly developed sense of timing is something of an understatement. Their lives depend on it.

Many of them wear a chronometer they call the best in the world. Its Oyster case is carved out of a solid block of 18 ct. gold or Swedish stainless steel. So much of the work is done by hand, each Rolex Oyster takes more than a year to make.

Jackie Stewart thinks it is time well spent. The Rolex he wears is the Datejust.

ROLEX
OF GENEVA

time, requiring the standardization of a range of movements of different sizes – an industrial, Fordist, high-level production line approach also new to the watch industry.

Within two years Wilsdorf had his company's first product and had underscored its reliability by successfully submitting it to the Official Watch Rating Centre, in Bienne, for its Swiss Certificate of Chronometric Precision. Four years later a Rolex watch was awarded a class-A precision certificate by London's Kew Observatory, a rating previously only given to the very best marine chronometers. But Rolex wasn't just about its accuracy or durability – it also remodelled the industry with its emphasis on wristwatches, or "wristlet watches" as Wilsdorf referred to them in the parlance of the day, betting as he did in 1914 that in time the demand for pocket watches would die out completely.

Wilsdorf commented that he felt he was taking something of a gamble, since the wristwatch was not a popular idea at the time – in part because it was, he said, "contrary to the conception of masculinity". But so few watchmakers thought it had a future also because of the challenges of reducing the size of a pocket watch movement to something that would fit on one's wrist, while also remaining as reliable as a pocket watch; and then also making it robust enough to take the impact of being so exposed to dust, damp and the occasional knock. But, Wilsdorf figured, if ever a wristwatch was going to find demand, it would be in England, "a country of sportsmen par excellence". He was to be proved right.

A MOVE TO SWITZERLAND

Rolex would probably have remained a British company – changing the course of watchmaking history as a result – were it not for the outbreak of the First World War. The heavy duties imposed on the export of luxury goods, and on the precious

OPPOSITE Rolex entered the watch market when the very idea of wearing a watch on the wrist – as opposed to carrying it in a pocket – was still a novelty.

metals used to make Rolex watches, were devastating for the company during the war years, such that recovery after the war's end seemed unlikely. And then there was the discrimination that Wilsdorf, as German-born, felt in Britain during this period. Such factors forced him to relocate to Geneva and start again. It was in Switzerland in 1919 that he registered his business, first as The Rolex Watch Company and then as Montres Rolex SA.

Rolex's new location was both secure and at the heart of the watch business. But it's as much the timing of the company's inception that played to its strengths. The interwar years, and especially the 1920s – before the Wall Street Crash of 1929 – was a period of huge creativity and innovation: from the television to the vacuum cleaner, water skis to the Band-Aid, frozen food to the traffic light, there was a demand for technological advance. And this included wristwatches too. When, in 1926, Rolex launched the world's first waterproof wristwatch, dubbed the Oyster for its hermetically sealed case, it was all in keeping with the spirit of the age.

But the period also further revealed Wilsdorf's talent for marketing. In October 1927 Mercedes Gleitze had become the first British woman to swim the English Channel. When he heard about a proposed second cross-Channel swim, later that month, Wilsdorf approached her to become, effectively, Rolex's first brand ambassador. She wore an Oyster on a ribbon around her neck for that second swim – and while the swim had to be abandoned after 10 hours, the Oyster at least emerged triumphant, still accurate. Wilsdorf wasn't about to let this fact pass unnoticed: he took out an advertisement on the front page of the *Daily Mail* newspaper for "the wonder watch that defies the elements". Rolex had made its mark. And it had got ahead of an industry that largely "persisted in clinging to the pocket watch as their chief product," as Wilsdorf noted.

OPPOSITE Rolex was quick to realize the potential of one of its watches as a gift, especially to mark a landmark birthday or significant occasion.

Ironically, this very idea of a watch that defied the elements played against what Wilsdorf himself had once regarded as the appeal of the wristwatch, both as a force for renewal within the Swiss industry and as a driver for increased sales. He contended that if the pocket watch was more of an heirloom, passed down the generations unchanged, the wristwatch, being more visible, would be subject to the changes of fashion. Wearers would want to update their model periodically. Men and women alike would want to have not just one but several, each to better go with their chosen attire.

Yet here was Wilsdorf creating watches that, precisely, strived not only to be above fashion but tough enough to take the knocks of daily life. He even created an aquarium display for his dealers' store windows, in which, alongside the fish, could be placed an Oyster.

MORE BIG IDEAS

The Oyster's success seemed to give Wilsdorf and Rolex the confidence to push forward with further technological and design leaps for its watches. While other manufacturers focused on incremental improvements to the accuracy of mechanical watch movements, Rolex took a more holistic approach, reconsidering the wristwatch in the round – how could it be more durable, more legible, more wearable, more functional? And, indeed, how could its airtight, dustproof and watertight qualities be further protected, by minimizing the need to wind the watch, for example?

To this end, Rolex had long used other manufacturers to make its movements – the Bienne-based Aegler, for example, was a long-time supplier, albeit that the movements were signed "Rolex", and the original Daytona came with movement made by Valjoux – but it nonetheless had its own ideas as to how these could be improved. Rolex advanced the self-winding movement – essentially by attaching to the watch mechanism a weight that rotated according to the kinetic energy produced by movement of the wearer's arm, winding the watch up as it did so. It was not a new idea – many watchmakers had tried similar approaches before, notably the eighteenth-century watchmaker Abraham-Louis Perrelet and Wilsdorf's contemporary, John Harwood. But Rolex perfected it – albeit while acknowledging in subsequent advertisements the essential contribution of Perrelet and Harwood.

BELOW Modern Rolexes, like this GMT-Master II, carry a brand motif along the bezel inner as a counterfeiting measure.

from the
TOP OF
THE WORLD

to the
BOTTOM
OF THE SEA

ROLEX *proves dependable!*

In the same year when the roof of the world was

at last conquered by the Rolex equipped Everest expedition,

the Rolex Company produced a special "Oyster" model watch, which, affixed outside

the Bathyscaphe "Trieste," submerged to 10,350 feet . . .

and after surfacing was in perfect condition . . . keeping perfect time.

With the new-found sports craze . . . "skin-diving" . . . and as a result of deep-sea testing, Rolex is now able to add to the equipment of skin-divers with a unique, new water-proof, pressure-proof watch . . . the "Submariner." This instrument has a special rotating bezel, enabling the user to determine elapsed time at a glance: for instance, it keeps a diver alert to how much time he has before his supply of air will run out. The "Submariner" has almost all the advantages of a stop watch with none of the complications. Unconditionally guaranteed against any water pressure . . . here is another truly incomparable Rolex masterpiece.

BE SURE TO WRITE FOR THE SPECIAL FREE BOOKLET ON THE ROLEX "SUBMARINER"

ROLEX

A Landmark in the History of Time Measurement

THE AMERICAN ROLEX WATCH CORPORATION · 580 FIFTH AVENUE · NEW YORK 19, N. Y.

That it achieved a reliable system was just as well, reckoned Wilsdorf. He reckoned that the reputation of the automatic movement was on the line. Various attempts to perfect this innovation so far proving unsuccessful, if Rolex then offered anything less than a precision solution the whole idea of the automatic movement might be dismissed once and for all by the industry and consumer alike.

Rolex called its system – designed by Rolex's technical chief-director Emile Borer – the "perpetual" rotor, and it's the foundation of automatic movements today. In 1945, at the end of the Second World War, Rolex unveiled the first watch with a date display – the Datejust. The model, with its distinctive serrated or "fluted" bezel and new bracelet, represented an aesthetic departure for most watches too.

During this period, the company even made pioneering forays into philanthropy, the death of Wilsdorf's wife, Florence, in 1944 prompting him to give his shares in the company, and a percentage of its profits, in perpetuity, to a foundation that would support various charities. That foundation owns and runs Rolex today.

THE CREATION OF CLASSICS

The 1950s would likewise bring a roster of more firsts in watchmaking from Rolex, not least the first diving watch, with the Submariner of 1953, waterproof to a then jaw-dropping 100m (328ft). This was just the first of the company's "tool" watches for professionals, an idea conceived by René-Paul Jeanneret, Rolex's then director of marketing and friend of the legendary underwater explorer Jacques Cousteau, who helped deliver the Submariner. These watches would be sold to professionals – divers, pilots, explorers and the like – but with added appeal to people who aspired to be like such professionals

OPPOSITE From the mid-1950s Rolex capitalized on its growing reputation for making tough "tool" watches, ably assisted by real world examples of them in action.

but who, in all likelihood, would not wear their diving watch any deeper than the bottom of the swimming pool on holiday.

The GMT-Master, for example, was developed primarily for pilots and reflected the decade's rapid growth in international air travel. In 1956 came both the Oyster Perpetual Day-Date, the first wristwatch to display both the date and the day of the week, and the Milgauss, which could resist magnetic fields of up to 1,000 gauss – enough to turn other mechanical watches haywire (see page 74). In 1957 Rolex made its first forays into watches for women by – ingeniously for the time, and challenging received wisdom about what women would wear – taking its unisex aesthetic and simply scaling it down for smaller wrists, something it did first with the Datejust. Men, however, were still expected to make the purchase. As one Rolex advertisement put it, noting the waterproof quality of Oyster watches: "Give your wife something to wear in the shower."

The 1960s marked further technological leaps for Rolex – and the end of an era. Wilsdorf died in 1960, leaving no heirs, and was succeeded after a three-year interim period by André Heiniger (who in turn was succeeded in 1992 by his son, Patrick). But that decade also brought a broader awareness of the brand. Rolex was developing watches for racing car drivers – the Cosmograph Daytona debuted in 1963, named after the Daytona International Speedway, the famed endurance driving venue – and for professional divers. It was fixing prototype watches to the side of submersibles, including the *Trieste* on its voyage 11,000m (36,000ft) down to the bottom of the Mariana Trench, the deepest point in the seas, an experiment that helped in the development of the Oyster Perpetual Sea-Dweller, launched in 1967 and waterproof to 610m (2,000ft).

But Rolex was also now gaining a cultural cachet, one that would only be underscored by the unexpected success of the

LEFT Elvis Presley takes a break during the filming of the 1962 movie *Girls! Girls! Girls!*, his Submariner teaming with the nautical style.

new James Bond film franchise. Sure, there had been some loose connection with celebrity before – Humphrey Bogart wore a Rolex Prince in the 1940 film, *They Drive By Night*.

Now famous fans of all stripes abounded: Elvis Presley would wear a Rolex in 1962's *Girls! Girls! Girls!*, while actor and serious car racing enthusiast Paul Newman embraced the Daytona – making for arguably the strongest ever association between a celebrity and specific model of watch. Picasso wore a Rolex, as did Cuban revolutionary Fidel Castro (who had a habit of wearing two at the same time), the US president Lyndon B. Johnson, Martin Luther King Jr. and the General Secretary of the Communist Party of the Soviet Union, Leonid Brezhnev. It was clear that a 1957 advertisement had it right: "Men who guide the destinies of the world wear Rolex watches."

The Rolex was coming to be associated as the choice of the elite. Dustin Hoffman was gifted a GMT-Master by a Rolex executive in the late 1960s and would go on to wear it for the next 20 years, both on set for films like *Marathon Man and Straw Dogs* and off. But not everyone wore their Rolex with such enthusiasm. John F. Kennedy was given a Rolex by Marilyn Monroe inscribed: "Jack, with love always, from Marilyn" – but he is said to have immediately passed it to one of his Secret Service detail, instructing the agent to dispose of it. The gift didn't see daylight until it was auctioned in 2005, long after his death.

CHANGING TIMES

Fortunately this popularity didn't sidetrack Rolex from its research and development programme of watches for professionals. The next decade, the 1970s, saw the launch of the Explorer II, with its distinctive orange 24-hour hand, and an even more impressive take on the professional diving watch, the Sea-Dweller 4000, now capable of functioning 1,200m (4,000ft) beneath the surface of the seas. But nor did Rolex become the world's biggest high-end watch brand by ignoring a golden opportunity either: the 1970s also saw its move into what it called Stella dial models, essentially sporty models but now also festooned with cut gems or exquisite lacquerwork. These were not models for adventurers, but they rode the first waves of bling.

That said, the timing for Rolex to achieve such status could not have been better. The 1970s were a challenging time for the Swiss mechanical watch industry, threatened by the advent of affordable, accurate and reliable quartz movements – pioneered in Switzerland but capitalized on by Japanese companies. Many watchmakers went under. Rolex was able to survive the storm, in part through its credibility – both as an innovator and a prestige

OPPOSITE The Sky-Dweller is (at the time of writing) Rolex's latest entirely new model, here in its proprietary Everose, a tarnish-proof rose gold alloy.

RIGHT Boldly coloured dials – known as Stella dials, after the company that provided the pigment and lacquer used – gave a contemporary freshness to otherwise function-driven designs.

brand. It could always count on, and capitalize on, being perceived as a luxury brand.

Inevitably perhaps, the period of the "Quartz crisis", as the industry called it, and the decades that followed, saw what was arguably a less bold company – certainly relative to its history of introducing benchmark transformations of the wristwatch. There was now a focus on the launch of new versions, or "references", of established models, maybe with upgraded parts or enhanced movements, or "calibres": the likes of the GMT-Master II, with its independent 24-hour hand, for example, or the Explorer II, an update of the Explorer. Remarkably, this approach – building on a solid basis of established classics and benchmark technologies rather than seeking to continuously reinvent the wheel – was Wilsdorf's stated intention from the beginning. As he noted in 1946, one of his core tenets was "to give current models the benefit of the results and improvements obtained with specially constructed high precision specimens" – evolution, not revolution.

This isn't to say original models were not created – 1992, for instance, saw it address another adventurous and upscale activity with a dedicated watch, through the introduction of the Yacht-Master, and in 2012 it introduced the Sky-Dweller, combining an annual calendar compilation – Rolex's first – with a dual time zone. That 20 years had passed between these two watches suggests just how reluctant Rolex became to release entirely new models. There had to be a very good reason for a new model – and that was not so often apparent.

Rather, it can be argued that much of the progress Rolex continued to make was less obvious. If Rolex made less radical advances in functionality with its watches, it now developed a reputation for driving a forward-looking approach to the proprietary materials from which its watches were made – the likes of Cerachrom or Everose. And, on the business front, it began its shift toward acquiring suppliers – the likes of Aegler, in 2004 – in order to become a vertically integrated company. It would come to make everything – excepting, at the time of writing, sapphire crystals and hands – in-house. Indeed, it began its shift to becoming the unassailable giant of Swiss watchmaking.

As Wilsdorf once put it: "We want to be first in the field and Rolex should be seen as the one and only – the best."

ALL IN THE FAMILY

ROLEX'S MOST IMPORTANT MODELS

Arguably Rolex has created more watches that have gone
on to become classics than any other watchmaker.
From the Submariner to the Datejust, these endlessly
copied models have helped define the modern timepiece.

OYSTER

When Mercedes Gleitze became the first British woman to swim
the English Channel, in 1927, her success was somewhat marred
when a hoaxer claimed to have made the swim before, and in a
faster time. So, just a fortnight later, Gleitze set out to swim the
21 or so miles (34km) again in what was dubbed the
Vindication Swim.

It was already receiving considerable publicity when Hans
Wilsdorf realized the promotional potential in the swim, and he
asked Gleitze to wear his Oyster. She didn't complete the second
crossing, needing to be pulled from the too-cold water 7 miles
(11km) short of the shore. At this point, a journalist from *The*

OPPOSITE The beautiful simplicity of an early Oyster Perpetual
with outsized crown; this vintage example is missing its sub-dial
second hand.

OPPOSITE Inside an early Rolex Oyster Perpetual – the rotor that ingeniously self-wound the watch clearly visible.

BELOW Did Edmund Hillary or Sherpa Tenzing wear their Rolex Oysters to the summit of Everest in 1953? Probably not. Yet the association lives on...

Times noted that "she was wearing a gold watch on a ribbon around her neck. It was still keeping perfect time". And so a legend was born.

One month after Gleitze's swim, the first Rolex Oyster was launched in the UK. Cartier had created what is now recognized as the first wristwatch in 1904 – for the aviator Alberto Santos-Dumont – and now wristwatches began to grow in popularity to replace pocket watches. Since they were so often being worn by adventurers, explorers and sportsmen for their practicality, Wilsdorf set about creating a new, deliberately tough option.

In 1910 Rolex's Oyster received the first official chronometer certification for a wristwatch; in 1922 the company launched what it called a Submarine (not Submariner) watch, so called because the glass screwed onto the caseback to close together in

the way a submarine hatch did, providing a hermetic seal. The same watch hid the winding crown within the case – an idea patented by one Jean Finger in 1921, and to which Wilsdorf bought the rights. This proved rather fiddly – but was the genesis for the fluted bezel that would become a signature of some later Rolex watches.

Rolex then bought the rights to the patent for an alternative method – a watertight screw-down crown, from Swiss prototype watchmakers Georges Perret and Paul Perregaux – and was able to improve on it with a modified design under its own patent. At last, Wilsdorf's dream for the Oyster could be realized. In 1926 the Oyster became the first dustproof, airtight and, most impressively for the time, waterproof watch ever made.

"It can, in consequence, be worn in the sea or bath without injury, nor would arctic or tropical conditions affect the wonderful precision of its beautifully poised movement," boasted an ad for the *Daily Mail*. The Oyster's launch, it continued, "introduces for the first time the greatest Triumph in Watchmaking". It "marks a unique development in the forwards stride of the chronomatic science…" Later that year, nearing December, further ads suggested shoppers "Make it a Rolexmas".

Some 27 years after its launch, the Oyster was still the hardiest watch on the market. That's why the British Expedition to conquer Everest in 1953 – led by Sir John Hunt, and during which Edmund Hillary and Tenzing Norgay summited the mountain – wore Oyster. By then, the larger hands introduced by Rolex for its sports models – Explorers and Submariners – would be referred to as Mercedes hands, in homage to Gleitze.

DATEJUST

The Datejust was launched to mark Rolex's 1944 jubilee. It was Rolex's largest watch to date and Wilsdorf was very pleased

OPPOSITE A 1965 Explorer – like the kind that went to the top of Everest, maybe – still with its signature 3–6–9 dial, which was at this time still printed.

with it. It was, as he called it, "a synthesis of all that has been achieved up to the present day."

What was the cause of such excitement? What was so different? It is hard to appreciate its novelty now that the idea is so commonplace, but the Rolex Datejust was, as advertising described at the time, "the only automatic, absolutely waterproof watch in which the date is shown through the small aperture without needing a special hand". One, furthermore, that would change automatically every night at midnight.

The movement also brought in what Rolex called an ingenious method of fixing the hairspring, such that "all danger of the coils being damaged by shock and causing mal-adjustment is eliminated" – a concern given the added complexity of a watch that displayed the date.

The Datejust was also the first of Rolex's classic, most

The Gift of Time.. Always

The Rolex "Jubilee" .. superb gem of the Swiss watch craftsman's skill .. is without peer to commemorate the rare occasion .. It is the first and only waterproof, self-winding wrist chronometer* to give the second .. the minute .. the hour .. the date. Individual numerals appear.. clearly.. through a small aperture .. which focuses on the daily change, without a distracting extra hand. • Encased in a design of individual elegance, it combines masculine beauty with the ultimate in technical ingenuity. Comes in a magnificent leather utility gift package.

The $1,000 "Jubilee"

ROLEX

Masterpiece of Watch Craftsmanship

A watch may be truly termed a chronometer after it has been certified by an Official Observatory Test made in five positions... and two temperatures. Every Rolex Chronometer is accompanied by an official certificate attesting to these facts.

At Christmas.. Graduation.. Anniversaries.. for the favored associate or retiring executive.. this rare gift is a heritage of pride. The incomparable wrist chronometer, its companion the Oyster Perpetual, and exquisite ladies' model illustrated, are available at exclusive jewelers only.

THE AMERICAN ROLEX WATCH CORPORATION   580 Fifth Avenue, New York 19, N.Y.

long-lived designs not to be created with a particular sport or activity in mind. And, in fact, it wasn't until the 1950s that Rolex appeared confident enough in the longevity of its creation to print "Datejust" on the dial. The Datejust also brought in what would become its signature serrated bezel and the debut of a new, five-piece bracelet style for Rolex, dubbed the Jubilee – a name that was at one point considered for the watch model itself. Bar variations in the size or calibre offered, the only major aesthetic change to the Datejust was, three years after its invention, the introduction in 1957 of the Cyclops date magnifier – a perfectly sensible addition given the model's name.

The Datejust would certainly come to have its lifelong fans – Harrison Ford, for example, was frequently snapped wearing his, both in character and off set. But in its earlier days Rolex was keen to connect the new watch – its most deliberate "lifestyle" or general-purpose model at that point – with figures of the times who might be considered generally pioneering.

David Sarnoff – who served on Dwight Eisenhower's communications staff during the Second World War and went on to build Radio Free Europe and then the US's colour TV network – was one such that Rolex connected with the Datejust in its advertising. And ads from the early 1990s feature Richard Adams, the archaeologist who discovered the ancient Mayan city of Rio Azul, noting that someone who works in such remote locations "must rely on whatever equipment he takes with him on a dig".

That such names are largely lost to history – at least relative to the statesmen and sporting greats with which Rolex also developed relationships – speaks to the essentially quiet, humble nature of the Datejust, often sidelined in assessments of Rolex's "greatest hits", and yet one of the company's biggest sellers.

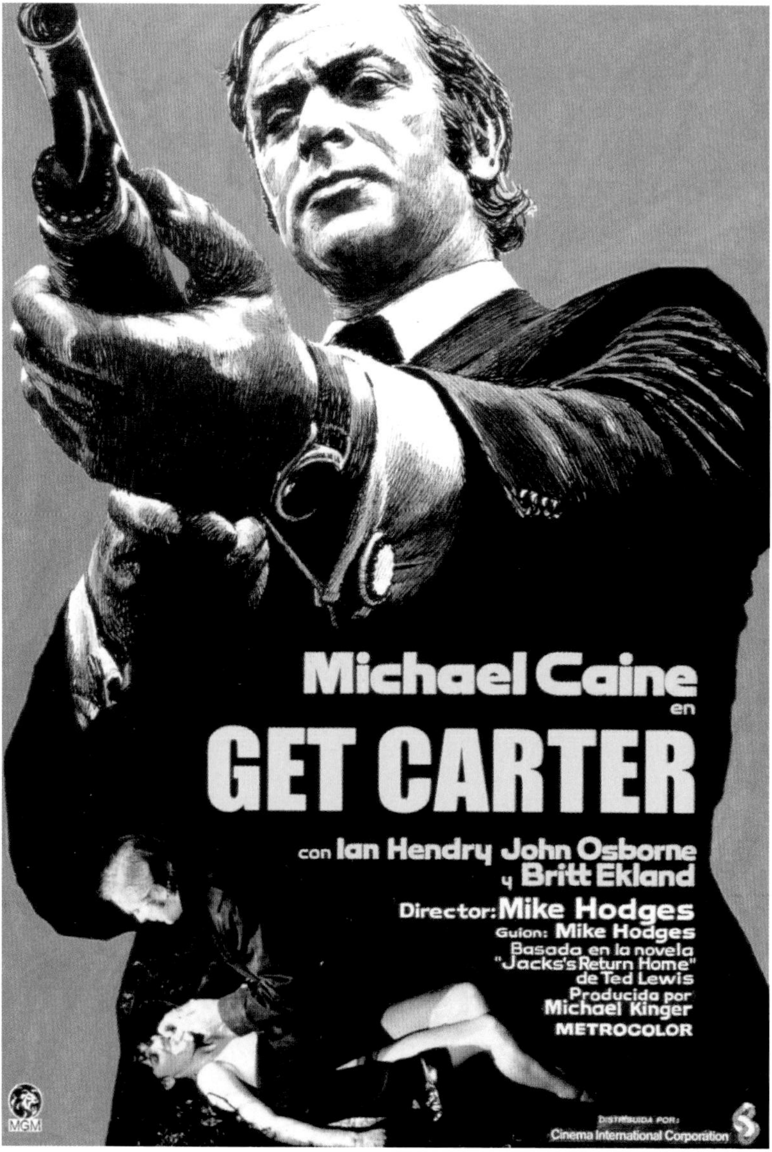

Michael Caine
en

GET CARTER

con **Ian Hendry John Osborne**
y **Britt Ekland**

Director: **Mike Hodges**
Guion: **Mike Hodges**
Basada en la novela
"Jacks's Return Home"
de Ted Lewis
Producida por
Michael Kinger
METROCOLOR

MGM

DISTRIBUIDA POR:
Cinema International Corporation

OPPOSITE In 1971's *Get Carter* the Datejust worn by Michael Caine's character symbolized his having "done good" in London before returning to his northern home town to avenge his brother.

RIGHT The actor Harrison Ford, here in 1984, has been a lifelong fan of the Datejust – even wearing it while woodworking, apparently.

OPPOSITE A rare
Day-Date with
Roman numeral
dial – as the
French indicates,
Rolex produced
the model for
various markets
internationally.

BELOW The Day-
Date was the first
wristwatch to
display, as its name
suggests, both day
and date; and the
first to be stamped
"superlative
chronometer".

DAY-DATE

It had been six years in development, the first patent for a watch that displayed both the day and date of the week in separate windows having been filed by Rolex in 1950, with a design credited to Rolex's Marc Huguenin. Six years later – and more patents filed – a watch with these complications (functions beyond displaying hours and minutes) was finally unveiled.

It wasn't just the display that made the Day-Date distinctive. While Rolex's core bracelets – the wide, three-piece link Oyster and the five-piece link Jubilee – have been used across many models and have helped make its watches stand out, the Day-Date came with its own design, one which has largely been used exclusively for this model ever since. It's a three-piece link bracelet comprising semi-circular links and a concealed "Crownclasp", in the shape of the Rolex logo. And it's only ever made in precious metal.

By the following year, a gently updated version of the Day-Date also became Rolex's first watch to have the words "Superlative Chronometer Officially Certified" on the dial, a phrase that would appear on many subsequent Rolexes. Actually, it was tested to twice the standard required to receive that certification.

But there was another, unofficial, label that came to be associated with the Day-Date: it's known as The President, with even the bracelet alone referred to as The President Bracelet. That nickname came about through the model being worn by so many US presidents, although not Dwight D. Eisenhower, who stuck with the Datejust Rolex sent to him in 1951 to commemorate his achievement as Supreme Commander of the Allied Forces during the Second World War. The following year he wore it prominently for a cover portrait for *Life*, then one of the most widely read magazines in the world, though later he had to return the watch for repair after it started to lose time – a result, he suggested, of wearing it while playing too much golf.

Rolex clearly knew that this growing association with the Oval Office was promotional gold but reacted rather coyly. One advertisement of 1956 – when Eisenhower was President – pictured him and his watch from behind, without stating who this figure was. "Because [such men] are so important they are, inescapably, the best known men in the world," it stated. "We cannot mention their names. It would not be fitting to do so, for they include royalty, the heads of States, great statesmen, service chiefs – the people who feel the pulse of our times. But the next time you see their pictures, take a look at something you might not normally notice – the watch on their wrists."

The subtext is clear: the most powerful people pick Rolex. Later versions of the ad stated that Rolex couldn't even publish a photo of them – let alone mention their names. Or it did

OPPOSITE Rolex's long association with the US presidency – notably with its Day-Date model – has seen the brand championed by the likes of Ronald Reagan.

52 ALL IN THE FAMILY

publish a photo and then used typography to block out the faces of these world leaders. But when Lyndon B. Johnson, US President from 1963 to 1969, favoured the Day-Date, his high visibility during the era that saw the birth of global mass media ensured the connection stuck. Such was the connection between the Day-Date and the Oval Office that the watch effectively came with the job – Ronald Reagan wore the model, as did Donald Trump. Trump did so before being elected.

Maybe the Johnson era convinced Rolex to open up on the subject – and, arguably, it was one of its advertisements during his terms of office that cemented the association between Day-Date and President. The creative work by ad agency J. Walter Thompson never stated directly that the US president wore the model, but pictured a hand holding a red phone – the direct line to the Kremlin perhaps – and stated bluntly that it was "the presidents' watch". Gerald Ford was the next President to do so and the first of many. Still, it wasn't until the 1980s that Rolex itself – still a touch coy – started to publicly refer to the watch as the President Day-Date.

EXPLORER

"We built the Rolex Explorer because there isn't any watch repair shop on the Matterhorn," ran a line from a 1970s advertisement. "This is the watch we engineered for the lonely places." The ad goes on to explain what, for the time, made the Explorer such a hardy piece of kit: that its case is carved out of a single block of Swedish steel, making the watch seamless; that it's tested at temperatures ranging from -46°C (-50°F) to 66°C (150°F), and underwater to a depth of 100m (330ft). And then the Swiss Institute for Chronometer double-checks its accuracy for 15 days and nights. "When a mountain climber says the best watch in the world is as tough as an alp," said another ad, "he's not joking."

The 1950s were the golden age of mountaineering and Rolex wanted to be part of it – such that in 1952 the company equipped a number of expeditions with 20 Oyster "bubbleback" watches – so nicknamed for their bulbous caseback, which housed the then typically deep automatic winding movement (these are also sometimes referred to as *ovettone*, an Italian phrase roughly translated as "big egg").

Among these expeditions were – as preparation for a summiting of Everest – climbs of Cho Oyu, a mountain some 20km (12 miles) from Everest, and among the climbers Alfred Gregory, Charles Evans and, most famously, the New Zealander Edmund Hillary – who would become, with Tenzing Norgay, the first to summit the world's tallest mountain the following year.

Contrary to all the myth-making – and myths help shore up the appeal of many watches from many makers – Hillary didn't wear his Oyster watch on the summit. He may have had it with him, or left it at base camp; the record isn't clear. He was almost certainly wearing a watch by the British watchmaker Smiths – though, to confuse matters, Hillary subsequently put his name to a Smiths advertisement in which he is quoted: "I carried your

OPPOSITE The less well-known Rolex Explorer II with a white dial, making it the so-called "polar" edition, here with lume in full effect.

watch to the summit. It worked perfectly." Carried it, that is, but didn't necessarily wear it…

By the time of the summit, though, Rolex was pressing ahead and making further improvements to its still unnamed, prototype "pre-Explorer" Oyster model, introducing a three-piece case that secured the crystal and, together with the addition of a screw-down crown, allowed it to be watertight – a necessary improvement given that the bubblebacks were found to let moisture in. And then came more changes which edged the mode to what would become its defining form: a 3-6-9 dial, the inverted triangle at 12 o'clock, Mercedes rather than pencil hands, and, finally, the addition of the word "Explorer" to the dial. This may or may not have been chosen as the name because Smiths already had an Everest model commercially available.

In 1956 an upgraded movement, the calibre 1030 and the very first that Rolex would make (almost) entirely in-house, would also allow the Explorer to be a flatter watch, while in 1963 the material used to give the dial markers their luminosity, radium, was replaced by tritium – as it was across all Rolex watches – after radium's radioactivity was recognized as harmful to health.

That wasn't the end of the Explorer model, though, nor of the Explorer name. In 1971 Rolex followed its Explorer with the Explorer II – with its distinctive 24-hour arrowhead hand in orange, indicating am/pm and (on later versions) a second time zone. The watch was designed with spelunkers, or cave explorers, in mind – hence luminous markers at each interval of five minutes, helpful for those in total darkness. But actually it became closely associated with another legendary climber, the Italian Reinhold Messner, the first person to summit Mount Everest without oxygen.

OPPOSITE
Remarkably, vintage watches fetch considerable sums at auction despite being in visibly distressed condition, like this 1978 Explorer II.

"In 1953 they used Rolex Oysters and oxygen," noted a Rolex advertisement, somewhat fudging the details. "In 1978 they managed without the oxygen." Again though, it's unclear whether Messner actually wore the Explorer II to the summit. He may have even worn a Rolex Oysterquartz – from the roughly 25-year period after 1970 when Rolex made watches with quartz movements – which he also favoured.

The Explorer II is also widely associated with Steve McQueen. There's no evidence that the actor ever wore one.

SUBMARINER

The Rolex Submariner might well be the most-copied watch ever, such is its status as a design icon, in no small part because it is the model that has undergone the fewest aesthetic changes over the years – essentially only the addition of Mercedes hands and a crown guard. No wonder it has "a cachet that is unmatched by any other watch" – and that's how the test pilot and NASA astronaut Scott Carpenter, one of the Mercury Seven, put it.

Developed in 1953 and launched the following year, the Submariner offered a functionality that, although commonplace now, was a breakthrough for the time. Of course, the watch

LEFT The earlier Rolex Submariners were rated to just 100m (330ft) – with improved technology, this was later increased to 200m (660ft), as with this model, and later the standard 300m (984ft).

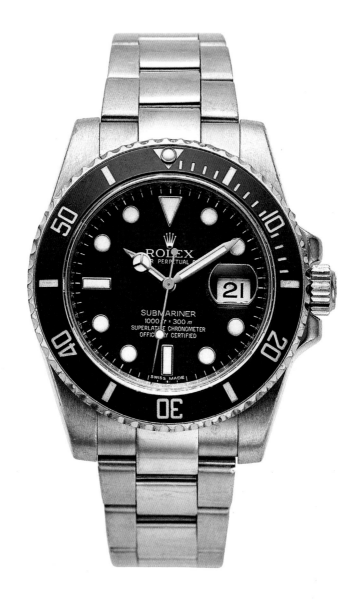

had to be waterproof to depth – 100m (330ft) for the first rendition – but it also had what Rolex called a "revolutionary time-recorder", better known today as the calibrated bezel that could be turned and set so zero matched with the minute hand and so display elapsed time underwater – essential for timing decompression stages to prevent "the bends". Or as Rolex described it, the Submariner offered "all the advantages of a stop watch with none of the complications".

The idea for the watch was said to come from René-Paul Jeanneret, Rolex's director of communications and a keen diver. This was at a time when diving was still very much a specialist activity – it was only a decade earlier, in 1942, that Jacques Cousteau and Émile Gagnan invented the Aqua-Lung, a breathing system that allowed for much longer spells spent underwater than previously possible. One Rolex advertisement of the period refers to the "new-found sports craze [of] 'skin-diving'".

Testing of Jeanneret's idea involved creating a prototype watch, a Deep Sea Special, attaching it to the side of the *Trieste*, the bathyscaphe piloted by the scientist and deep sea explorer Jacques Piccard. The watch was taken down to almost 3,132m (10,275ft) and, on return, tested for function. It was found to be in perfect order. This led to a longer series of tests at shallower depths by the Institute for Deep Sea Research in Cannes, which pulled the stops out – literally. The prototype was dunked with the crown pulled out, for example – still there was no water ingress and the watch ticked on. It was even successfully tested 20m (65ft) below its rated resistance.

OPPOSITE What else to nickname this Submariner, with bold purple-blue dial and bezel? Royal? Azure? No, "Smurf", of course...

The Submariner – at one point both "Skin Diver" and "Sub-Aqua" were considered for its name – would not be the first diving watch. There was the Omega Marine of 1932 – the first commercially available – and, shortly after, Panerai's Rolex-

count: this 1958 "Big
Crown" Submariner
is all the rarer for its
red triangle, four-
line topography
and, more subtly
still, the outsized
crown.

BELOW The Rolex
Deep Sea Special
watch that went
to the bottom
of the Mariana
Trench, a depth of
11,000m (36,000ft,
or almost 7 miles),
withstanding
pressure of seven
tons per square
inch.

made, military-only Radiomir. Nor was it the first to respond
to this new era of diving: Blancpain launched its Fifty Fathoms
model just a few months before Rolex did its Submariner.
Blancpain also held the patent for the unidirectional bezel too –
one that could be turned in only one direction, so that if it was
accidentally moved it would indicate only that divers had less
time than they thought.

But then Rolex arguably had the edge in holding the patent
for a winding crown with special gasket – the Twinlock crown
as it was called – which virtually guaranteed no water could
get inside the movement. And crucially, at least as far as profile
and public perception went, it would also have the backing
of one James Bond, a patronage that ensured the Submariner
would come to be regarded more as a style item for its largely
landlubber customers. Certainly, when Rolex added a date
function in 1974, it was all but admitting as much – as was
pointed out at the time, serious divers have little need to know
what the date is.

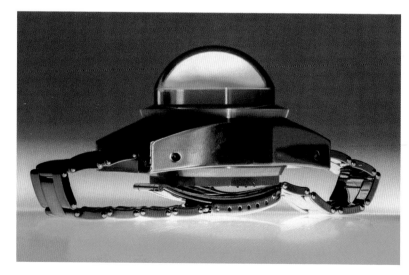

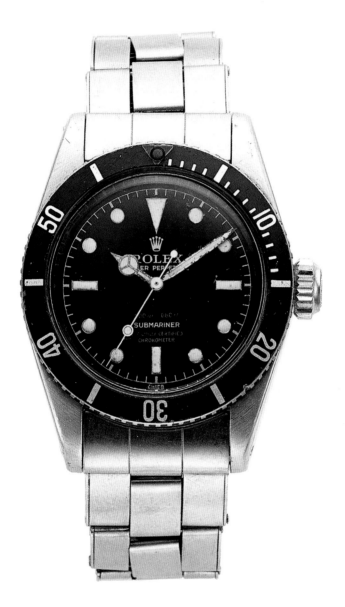

DAYTONA

Different people find appeal in different Rolex watches. But among collectors, and specifically those who collect watches as an investment on which they expect a return some day, the Daytona Cosmograph is not only the hardest to find – there is a long waiting list for this who want to buy one new – it is then also the most sought after. And this is despite Rolex having done next to nothing to promote the model for decades.

Incredibly, Rolex more or less gave up promotion of the watch after sales became so low that the model was effectively sidelined. Then a turn of events meant that no promotion was necessary: the reference 6239 Daytona had simply become the stuff of myth. And this is before actor Paul Newman's own Daytona set (what still stands at the time of writing) the world record for the price achieved at auction for the sale of a watch.

The Daytona was symbolic of Rolex's relationship with racing cars – one that, given the shared emphasis on mechanical complexity, has long seen watches and automotive engineering make easy bedfellows. The precision both required was something that Hans Wilsdorf much admired, especially in German cars with their reputation then for technical excellence: for much of his life he used a chauffeur-driven Mercedes and, despite Rolls-Royce's attempts to persuade him, would not deviate from his loyalty to that carmaker.

Furthermore, one of the company's first forays into celebrity endorsement was with Malcolm Campbell, following his 1935 breaking of the land speed record – and five of the nine land speed records that Campbell broke between 1924 and 1935 were at Daytona Beach in Florida, surely planting the seed for a future watch name.

If Campbell moved his efforts to Utah for his final land speed runs, Daytona Beach nonetheless remained the hub of American racing, at least for the winter season. The first stock-car race was held at Daytona, in 1936, and in 1938 racing car driver William France took over the site's management as president of NASCAR – and subsequently appeared in advertisements for the stainless steel and gold Rolex Zephyr.

But before the Rolex Daytona there was the stainless steel

OPPOSITE Such was the initial lack of demand for Rolex's Daytona that they were regularly given as race prizes – here, Pedro Rodriguez receives a watch for winning the Daytona Continental 3-Hour Race in 1963.

Oyster Chronograph, a model Rolex would later call the
Cosmograph. Its manual-wind reference 6234 version was made
only between 1955 and 1961 and is now widely seen as the
automatic Daytona's progenitor.

The watch was a beauty and tapped into a growing interest
in racing, even if its naming was confused – Rolex would refer
to its Chronograph also as the Cosmograph, and from 1962
there were versions of the Daytona with and without "Daytona"
printed on the dial.

And there is more confusion: in 1964 Rolex appeared to
rename the watch the Le Mans, in association with the famed
French 24-hour endurance race. And then in early 1965 it
was calling the model just the Rolex Cosmograph – "a highly
accurate masculine watch and a precision stop watch… for the
sports enthusiast and the businessman", as one advertisement
that year described it – and by the end of the year it was back to
calling it the Daytona, "after the International Speedway where
Rolex is the official timepiece". "Daytona", it seemed, would
finally stick.

Yet, for all of this chopping and changing, it was Paul
Newman's association with the Daytona that revived the model's
standing, and then made it the holy grail for vintage Rolex
fanatics. Newman was given his first Daytona as a gift from his
wife, Joanne Woodward – "Drive carefully, Me" was engraved on
the caseback – and his being regularly photographed wearing it
at races for the next 15 years only further enhanced the model's
profile and desirability.

In 1984 Newman gave his Daytona – the record-setting one
– to one lucky guy called James Cox, the college boyfriend of his
daughter, Nell. Thirty-three years later Cox consigned it to the
Phillips auction house for sale, promising to donate some of the
proceeds to philanthropic efforts in honour of Newman.

GMT-MASTER

"Simultaneously – local time at any two places anywhere in the world" – that, as Rolex put it, was the simple premise for the benefit of its GMT-Master, the watch launched in 1955 with Submariner styling but, thanks to the input of two "world-renowned" aviation companies, with a second hour hand that could display a second time zone. Or, at least, one that was a fixed number of hours apart. Destinations that were so many hours-and-a-half apart, for example, would require some additional mental arithmetic.

Nonetheless the model was chosen as the official timepiece of the American airline Pan Am – the first airline to offer an international service – because, as one advertisement of 1955 had it, "an airline's reputation depends upon its efficient scheduling – that's why Rolex has been chosen".

According to what is probably an apocryphal story, executives at Pan Am were said to have been issued with an exclusive version of the GMT-Master with a white-dial – Rolex sometimes made prototypes with white dials, but a white dial GMT-Master was never made commercially available – while pilots were issued the standard black dial.

William "Pete" Knight, the US Air Force pilot and later NASA astronaut, who in 1967 set the Mach 6.7 speed record for level flight in his X-15a – essentially a rocket with stubby wings – opted for the black-dial version too; as did Wally Schirra, the Mercury and Apollo astronaut.

BELOW If Rolex's "tool" watches lend themselves to function first, that still leaves room for creative embellishment – as with this 2019 GMT-Master II, complete with meteorite dial.

OPPOSITE Rolex
fans often give the
company's watches
unofficial names:
here, the GMT-
Master II "Batman",
so called for its
blue-black bezel.

Certainly, for all that the Omega Speedmaster may be the watch most closely associated with NASA – having passed various assessments to be officially adopted by the administration for its crews, and the moon missions in particular – it's easy to make the case that the GMT-Master was nonetheless the astronaut's choice. Jack Swigert and Jim Lovell – of *Apollo 13* "Houston, we have a problem" fame – wore the watch, as did all astronauts on the *Apollo 14* mission. Edgar Mitchell even wore two, one of which – so he said – he wore during what would become the all-time record for a moonwalk, at over nine hours. Ron Evans and Eugene Cernan, astronauts on *Apollo 17*, the last moon mission (so far), each wore a GMT-Master too. Given all this, it's hard to argue that the Rolex watch isn't as much a part of space history as the Speedmaster.

More grounded explorers also opted for the GMT-Master. Tom Sheppard, for one, had adopted the model with his first major desert expedition in 1967, and again in 1975 when he led a joint services expedition across the Sahara Desert, from west to east, including the first ever crossing through the then uncharted Mauritanian Empty Quarter. Thor Heyerdahl, and his crew, wore the GMT-Master for his experimental sailings of the 1970s, during which he tested whether historic methods of boatbuilding – using papyrus reeds, for example – could make the transoceanic trips that some historians suggested were impossible. Likewise it was the choice of Jeff MacInnis for the first sailing through the Northwest Passage in 1991.

Of course, most fans of the model were not explorers of this calibre. A large part of the appeal of the GMT-Master has always been its distinctive – and much-copied – look. The watch was not the first dual timezone watch – that was the Glycine Airman – but it was certainly identifiable at a distance, thanks to its distinctive two-colour, red and blue bezel – dubbed "Pepsi" by collectors, after the same shades used by the drinks company, or the later "Coke" variety in red and black. (Rolex would also create an "espresso" version with a Submariner-like, all-black bezel, and a black and blue one, which collectors quickly dubbed "The Batman", after the superhero's costume.)

This helped make it a style choice for the likes of Dizzy Gillespie, who proudly wore his for the next 30 years, Che Guevara and Fidel Castro, Marlon Brando and Clint Eastwood, whose rare, root beer-coloured version is his own but has made appearances in several films. And, as off screen, so on it: arguably it was Tom Selleck, as *Magnum P.I.*, who through the 1980s gave the watch its chance to outshine even the show's other design icon, a Ferrari 308 GTS.

OPPOSITE This 1999 GMT-Master II has a Coke bezel (as in Coca-Cola) in black and red – as opposed to the Pepsi in blue and red.

BELOW Even champions of communism can appreciate a Rolex – on occasion, Cuba's revolutionary leader Fidel Castro would wear two at a time.

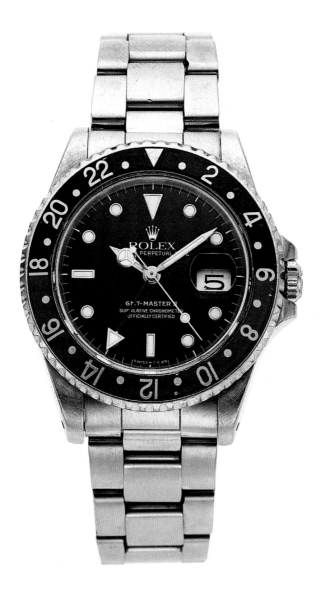

MILGAUSS

BELOW The lightning rod second hand, the dauphine hour/minute hands, the tessellated dial and Art Deco-style indices – for a scientific instrument some versions of the Milgauss were replete with decoration.

It's one thing to protect a watch from dust or water. Contact with either will not be good news for movement of a mechanical watch. But there's an invisible force that, if strong enough, will do even more damage: magnetism. So wearing a standard mechanical watch at, for example, CERN – the European Organization for Nuclear Research, founded in Geneva in 1954 – would not be wise. And especially in more recent times. For there is now housed the 100-tonne ATLAS Barrel Toroid, launched in 2006 and the largest superconducting magnet made to date. But then CERN might, conversely, also be exactly the place where you might need a

watch that was designed to protect its movement against the influence of magnetism – a watch like Rolex's Milgauss.

The Milgauss was initially a very limited edition watch – fewer than 100 examples of the first variant were made – and was introduced the year of CERN's foundation. The first two years saw variations with or without a Submariner-style spinning bezel, and with or without a dust cover inside the case back, with only versions from 1956 having what would become its design signature – a lightning bolt-style second hand.

But while most mechanical watches will operate well in magnetic fields of up to 60 or 70 gauss, all Milgauss models were created to withstand magnetic fields of up to 1,000 gauss – the unit of an object's magnetic induction intensity, named for physicist Carl Friedrich Gauss. This characteristic made the watch ideal for those conducting certain kinds of scientific or engineering work, or those working in medicine. "Milgauss" came from combining *mille* – French or Italian for "thousand" – with gauss.

The 1950s were viewed at the time as being a new scientific age – "where the rocket, the orbiting satellite and even journeys to the moon are the subjects of ordinary conversation," Rolex noted – and this was the watch for the pioneers of that age. The watch, it said proudly, "was exhaustively tested in the Philadelphia research laboratories of a leading electronics company". Other watchmakers – IWC, Omega, Jaeger-LeCoultre, Patek Philippe – subsequently launched their own anti-magnetic watches over the decade.

One thousand gauss is not particularly strong, relatively-speaking – an MRI scanner, which contains the strongest magnets in regular use, would run at 20,000 to 70,000 gauss. But magnets with a strength in the high hundreds would be found in all sorts of sensors, motors and measuring devices.

RIGHT The earlier Milgauss models borrowed the Submariner-style bezel to allow the scientist market at which they were aimed to record elated time.

OPPOSITE The Milgauss went in and out of production, but, with its two-colour lume and lightning second hand, is one of the most distinctive Rolex models.

The protection the Milgauss afforded against these came by applying the principle of the Faraday cage, encircling its movement in a soft iron band and, on later models, encasing the entire movement in a soft iron case within the watch case.

The Milgauss was a professional watch, much as the Submariner was a professional watch for divers. But whereas waterproofing to depth might appeal to non-professionals too, defending against magnetic forces inevitably had less everyday attraction. Subsequently, for all that Rolex produced the Milgauss with the workers at CERN in mind, the Milgauss never sold well, and in the end they were even given as prizes for winners of NASCAR and Daytona 500 races. The Milgauss was eventually discontinued in 1988, though it was reintroduced in 2007 – with a notable two-colour lume (luminous material) and green-tinged crystal – and then discontinued again in 2023.

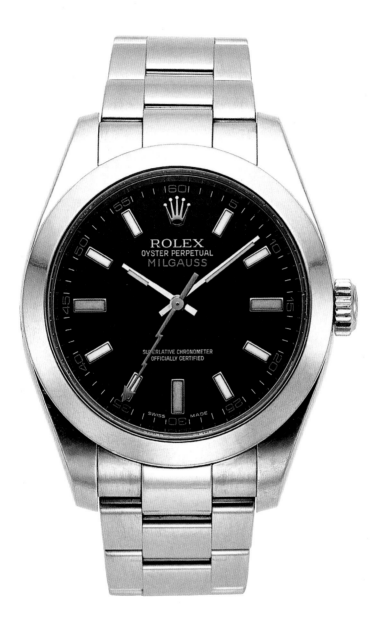

CELLINI

Rolex has since the 1940s been best-known as a manufacturer of robust, no-nonsense watches – designed for purpose, built to last. But with its Cellini line, named after the sixteenth-century Italian master goldsmith Benvenuto Cellini, it has also enjoyed a less prominent but still successful parallel life as a purveyor of purely luxury objects – expressions of craft, materials, finishing and gem-setting rather than utility or performance, of fashion rather than function. That Rolex could lead this parallel life was the vision of André Heiniger, who succeeded Hans Wilsdorf as Rolex's CEO in 1963. "Rolex," he is said to have intoned, "is not in the watch business. We are a luxury business."

One of Heiniger's first moves would be to call on the talents of independent watch designer Gerald Genta to create one of Rolex's most distinctive dress watches, the gold, hand-wound King Midas, launched in 1964. Genta would, over his career, design any number of watch classics – IWC's Ingenieur, Patek Philippe's Nautilus and Audemars Piguet's Royal Oak among them – and the King Midas was distinctly characterful too: a plain, refined two-hand dial set into an asymmetric, pentagonal engraved case, with the winding crown shaped like a stylized sun, and placed on a minimalistic gold link band.

It was, at the time, the heaviest gold watch commercially available – and Rolex's most expensive – and the first with a synthetic sapphire crystal glass, something that would appear on almost all Rolex watches subsequently. It was not, however, waterproof – Elvis Presley damaged his King Midas by wearing it in the bath. Somewhat counter to his swaggering public image, John Wayne wore a King Midas too, as did Francisco Scaramanga, the villain in the James Bond film *The Man with the Golden Gun*.

Jake Ehrlich, an unofficial but respected historian of Rolex

OPPOSITE Rolex's Cellini line of watches belies its reputation as a maker first and foremost of "tool" watches, but the results, here in 18-carat gold, can be stunning.

ABOVE Rolex's reputation for robust sports watches belies its talent for classical dress watches too, as embodied in the Cellini line.

watches, has argued that Genta's watch may not have been classified as a Cellini – not at first, at least – but its striking difference from what Rolex usually produced was probably the driving inspiration behind the launch, in 1968, of what would become the extremely diverse if sparse family of solid gold or platinum dress watches under the Cellini name.

This family would prove a site of experimentation in non-traditional dress watch design and produced the likes of the octagonal Cellini Octagon, during the 1980s, or the vintage-look Cellini Danaos of the 1990s. Over the decades since, Rolex at times barely kept the Cellini line extant, but its output was always welcomed as a sleek, streamlined and shiny counter to the company's Oyster-cased collections.

SEA-DWELLER

Rolex's underwater adventures, begun in the early 1950s with the Submariner, would continue into the 1960s with the Sea-Dweller. In 1960 the same experiment undertaken with the Submariner was repeated for another Deep-Sea Special, only this time the watch descended on the side of the bathyscaphe *Trieste* to the bottom of the Mariana Trench, at 11,000m (36,000ft or almost 7 miles) the deepest point on Earth. This was the first time anyone had gone to the bottom of the deepest ocean. Again, the prototype watch survived the journey and ended up displayed in The Smithsonian in Washington DC.

Although the incredible journey would prove a selling point for the Submariner, it also inspired the development of what, in

LEFT To Rolex collectors, a watch carrying the stamp of the French deep sea diving company COMEX, like this 1977 Sea-Dweller, is among the most desirable.

effect, was an enhanced deep-sea Submariner for more specialist use, the model that would come to be called the Sea-Dweller. This was not least because members of the SEALAB missions, the US Navy's attempt at the underwater equivalent of the Apollo moon missions, found that during decompression the build-up of helium gas within their Submariners had a habit of making the crystal pop off. Some would explode.

One of the SEALAB team, Bob Barth, suggested Rolex develop a diving watch with a helium escape valve, to prevent this happening. It would decompress at the same time as the diver wearing it. From 1967 first Sea-Dwellers – dubbed "single red" for their single line of red dial typography – had a greater depth rating than the Submariner, 500m (1,640ft) as opposed to 200m (660ft), but still no helium escape valve despite Rolex applying for a patent for just that the same year.

Rolex did, however, retrofit a helium escape valve onto one prototype Sea-Dweller to be worn by Professor Ralph Brauer, the leading researcher into the hyperbaric oxygen treatment of diving-related illness, and the man who pioneered the use of hydrogen as a breathing gas to counter the tremors sometimes caused by too-rapid decompression, a study he undertook by making himself the guinea pig. Something of a man of mystery, Brauer also headed a branch of the US military's investigations into applied nuclear research – which didn't stop him becoming the only American invited to take part in the Soviet Union's own deep-sea programme, during which time he covertly took photographs for the CIA.

If, over the 1960s, Omega had – officially at least – watches for the NASA space programme all sewn up, Rolex was all the more keen to claim ownership of the deep-sea diving world of these aquanauts and oceanauts. Indeed, Brauer would wear the watch on the 1968 COMEX Hydra project in Europe

OPPOSITE "Double red" may have significance only for hardcore collectors, but for them, those two lines of red dial typography set this 1972 Sea-Dweller above the rest.

ABOVE Rolex's association with the SEALAB II Project for deep-sea exploration allowed it to test its watches in real-world diving scenarios.

– COMEX being the French dive specialists with whom Rolex often worked to develop its diving models – despite the company at the time being contracted to Omega. Brauer, though, was under no such contract. The watch's gas release valve proving successful on the watch worn by him, Rolex then retrofitted its 1967 "single red" Sea-Dwellers for the subsequent SEALAB 3 Habitat mission.

It would take several tweaks to prototypes – including the development, from scratch, of a model that integrated the valve technology – before, in 1971, the Sea-Dweller became the first watch launched with Rolex's then still patent-pending valve technology for civilian use. In 2008 Rolex launched the chunkier, even more specialist Deepsea Sea-Dweller, and its first titanium watch, the Deepsea Challenge, able to withstand pressures at incredible depths of 3,900m (12,800ft) and 11,000m (36,090ft) respectively. And that later figure is as deep as you can go.

YACHT-MASTER

As the Submariner suggests life below the waves, and the GMT-Master well above them, so the Yacht-Master – to combine the two – aims at life on the ocean surface. Indeed, the Yacht-Master, introduced in 1992, was something of a mash-up of previous models, taking cues from many and synthesizing them into something fresh but also, clearly, belonging to the world of Rolex.

In fact, not only was Yacht-Master an old model name for Rolex – originally it was applied to a chronograph model that looks as though it belongs in the Daytona family – but the 1992 watch was conceived as an update to the Submariner before the Sea-Dweller was developed, but the Sea-Dweller was launched to market first.

BELOW The Yacht-Master was pitched in 1992 effectively as a deliberately more opulent design that capitalized on Rolex as a luxury brand as much as a watch brand.

Maybe the proposed Submariner update – with its etched bezel insert, bolder hands and metal-lined hour markers – was considered too radical a departure at the time, so the diving watch and its iconographic style was left alone – even if later models of the Submariner, after 2011, would extensively borrow the design language of the Yacht-Master for a harder, more sharply defined look, such that there wasn't much too different, aesthetically speaking, about the two watches.

Indeed, the Yacht-Master, when it was finally launched, was effectively positioned as an upscale version of the Submariner – sharing its movement too – with some of the earliest versions coming, for example, in 18-carat yellow gold with a white dial and later ones with ruby or sapphire set hour markers, or with dial and bezel in platinum. This made the dial harder to read than one with a more functional high contrast – but, while officially one of Rolex's professional line of watches, functionality wasn't really the point. Rather, the Yacht-Master blurred the lines between the Submariner's strict *form follows function* ethos and something much dressier – a sports watch for sportsmen to wear to the awards gala. Maybe Superyacht-Master is a more fitting description.

Much as Rolex would – in a break with convention – combine steel and gold on some models, a design it calls Rolesor, so with the Yacht-Master models it would combine monochromatic steel and platinum, which it refers to as Rolesium. In fact, Rolesium is, to date, used by Rolex only with Yacht-Master models. A Yacht-Master model would, in 2015, also be Rolex's first to break away from leather straps or its more signature bracelets. The Oysterflex strap looked like it was made of rubber, but, being Rolex, was actually a titanium nickel alloy blade with a black polymer coating.

OPPOSITE The Yacht-Master was Rolex's first new watch in 20 years when launched in 1992, readily identifiable by its combination of Everose and steel.

THE
APPLIANCE OF
SCIENCE

ROLEX, TECHNOLOGY AND MATERIALS

Hans Wilsdorf's second wife, Betty Wilsdorf-Mettler, couldn't see the date display on her watch. What, Rolex wondered, might be the solution? It turned out to be just another design detail on watches from a company that has been all about the details – but an ingenious one, nonetheless, and one that has gone on to become something of a signature for the brand.

A 2.5× magnifier window was built into the crystal, sitting over the date aperture and nicknamed the Cyclops, after the one-eyed giant of Greek mythology. The charm of the story may be greater than its veracity, but the idea is said to have come to Wilsdorf as he was washing one morning and a drop of water fell onto his watch right over the date display. So the company that invented the date display – with its Datejust model of 1945 – went on to create an improved means of using it three years later.

OPPOSITE Even if the techniques and technologies have advanced, manufacturing Rolex watches has always involved precision handcraft.

RIGHT Rolex has stamped bracelet clasps with the term Steelinox – "inox", an abbreviation of the French, meaning stainless – for watches made with both 316L steel and its more corrosion-resistant 904L steel.

It was such a simple, elegant yet easily copied solution that after 1953, when Rolex was granted the patent, the company was having to warn other watchmakers that the Cyclops was its idea and that it would take legal action against them if necessary. Indeed, Rolex would go on to add a Cyclops – later with a double anti-reflective coating for extra legibility – on almost every model it produced with a date display, in some cases to the consternation of purist fans.

The Cyclops was just another instance of an engineering advance for which Rolex would be well-known. If it was reluctant to introduce a brand-new model, preferring subtle upgrades to existing ones, it trumpeted the progress in how its watches were made. The first and most famous instances of this, of course – not least because variations on the themes would become standard across all mechanical watches – was the waterproofing of the Oyster.

Just as famous is the creation of its Perpetual automatic movement. This idea wound the movement using a rotor weight, such that, assuming the watch is worn every day for six hours – as was originally recommended – no manual winding should be required. Accurate time display would be "perpetual". Patented in 1931, Rolex's self-winding movement was initially produced outside the company as a module that could be affixed to existing movements – this would make the watch thicker than usual too, leading to the bubbleback style of caseback by which pre-war Rolexes are identified. The first purpose-made Oyster Perpetual movement did not come until 1950 – used in early versions of the Explorer or Submariner – though by the end of that decade it was standard in all Rolex models without date display.

But while the most important, the watertight Oyster and the Perpetual automatic movement were certainly not alone in what is a long list of Rolex's advances in watchmaking. Look on the dial of a Rolex in low light, for example, and its visibility is the result of the company developing its own luminescent material.

Like most watch manufacturers seeking to give their watches utility in the dark, Rolex initially used radium, a radioactive material. In 1963, however, the US Atomic Energy Commission wanted details: exactly how radioactive was the GMT-Master, with a dial and bezel both made from radium? This was a challenge that resulted in Rolex not only recalling the model from the US market, and swapping in aluminium bezels, but also exploring ways to stop using radium altogether.

Tritium was chosen, a material much less radioactive but also less long-lasting – which is why vintage Rolexes tend to lose their glow – and are prone to a yellow-brown discoloration over time. This is loved by vintage Rolex enthusiasts, but was considered a fault by Rolex itself. Consequently, in 1998 the company switched to LumiNova, a non-radioactive, typically green-tinged material created in 1993 by Nemoto & Co and now, alongside upgraded Super-LumiNova, the watch industry standard choice.

But then, in 2008, Rolex announced the blue-tinged Chromalight, a luminous material seemingly developed in-house, which debuted on a Deepsea Sea-Dweller, arguably the company's most specialist timepiece. Here was a luminous material that, Rolex claimed, glowed faster in low light conditions and for longer than Super-Luminova. Or, at least, that is what the secretive Rolex said – at the time of writing it remains inconclusive whether Chromalight is a propriety material, a propriety application of a non-proprietary material or just some clever re-branding of a LumiNova product.

That is certainly not the case for other Rolex advances, however. Look inside a Rolex watch and you will find the Parachrom Bleu hairspring, the development of which represented another step toward the company making almost the entirety of its products in-house.

The hairspring is an almost microscopically thin coil of wire that keeps the balance wheel oscillating at a precise rate, locking and unlocking the escapement's pallet fork, which in turn progresses the watch's hands. Originally made of steel, hairsprings could be negatively affected by changes in temperature and magnetism, making timekeeping unreliable. Hence both the development of specialist alloys over the early twentieth century – Invar, Elinvar and Nivarox among them

– and specialist manufacture for hairsprings, such that Rolex would buy in this part for its watches.

But Rolex also concluded – as it perhaps had with luminescent material – that what was available could also be improved on, and in 2000 it launched its own hairspring alloy, five years in development. Made of 15 per cent zirconium and 85 per cent niobium – valued for resisting wear, heat and oxidization when exposed to air – the alloy allowed the hairspring to be completely anti-magnetic, extremely resistant

ABOVE A work of art in miniature: the signed mechanism of a Rolex watch, with its proprietary Parachrom Bleu hairspring visible.

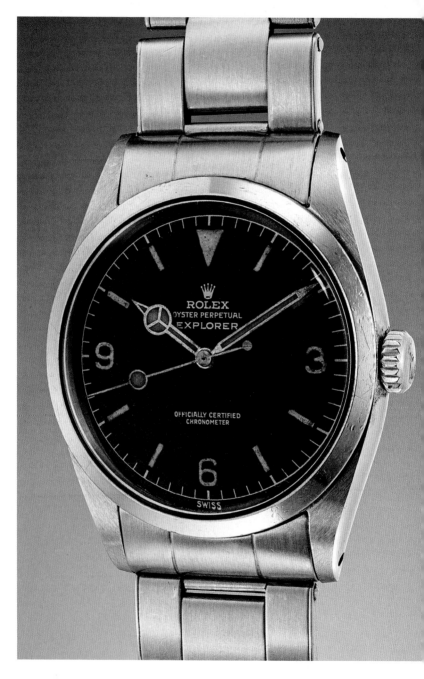

to temperature changes and, said Rolex, 10 times more shock-resistant. In 2005 Rolex's scientists would actually thicken the oxide later on its hairspring in order to give it greater stability, a process with the side effect of turning the hairspring blue.

To even be able to make a hairspring from this alloy required working at tolerances of around one-tenth of a micron – that's around one-thousandth the diameter of a human hair – and, to bond zirconia and niobium together, temperatures of about 2,400°C (4,352°F). But Rolex, ever keen to maximize control – and hence the high standards – of its production, had its own foundry and die presses in order to do this. In other words, the heart of twenty-first century Rolex watches would be the result of a heavy industrial process – but one Rolex managed to operate with extreme precision. A hairspring that is "off" by just one micron – a millionth of a meter – can produce a mechanical watch that runs fast or slow by as much as 30 minutes a day. Rolex claims its watches will, on average, run fast or slow by only around plus or minus two seconds a day.

Since Rolex did not make crystal casebacks, such wizardry was not for Rolex wearers to see. But that in-house foundry would also allow the company to reconsider the very materials from which its cases and bracelets were made. That applies to even its most humble steel models. Back in 1985 it switched from using the steel alloy 316L – widely used across the watch industry – to 904L steel, a type more expensive and harder to machine, and more typically used in the necessarily very safety-conscious aerospace industry. Rolex started to make its own formulation of this steel and would switch its entire production to 904L – or what was later dubbed Oystersteel – in 2003. Why 904L steel? Because it's harder, but, more importantly for any long-lived metal product, also more corrosion-resistant, and gives a brighter polish too.

OPPOSITE A Rolex Explorer, highlighting here the much-copied three-link Oyster bracelet – Rolex has succeeded in making its bracelet designs as distinctive as its watches.

OPPOSITE The use
of ceramic for Rolex
watch bezels, as on
this Yacht-Master,
also allowed the
numbers to be
raised for a more
sculptural effect.

As for glitzier models, Rolex controls its own platinum and gold production and has sought to bring a functional advantage to these too by producing proprietary alloys – of a secret formulation – that makes for a gold with a more distinctive, richer colour, and a platinum – mixed with ruthenium to make what Rolex called Rolesium – which is harder-wearing without losing its brilliance. Rolex would also create the likes of Everose in 2005, its rose gold alloy designed not to lose its particular shade as a result of long exposure to sunlight, saltwater or chlorine.

And while steel or precious metals have long been the traditional materials from which watch cases and bracelets are made – appreciated for their durability, lustre and status – Rolex also embraced the potential of new materials to produce parts that are, for example, lighter in weight but also (unlike aluminium) don't scratch, don't fade and hold bolder colour too. To this end, for example, in 2005 it patented a ceramic compound called Cerachrom – *cera* from "ceramic", *chrom* from the Greek for "colour" – for the manufacture of sports model bezels, which it then coated in a very thin layer of platinum to give a high gloss finish. The effect is best appreciated on any model with a "Pepsi" bezel since the ceramic allows the two colours to be joined flawlessly.

SHIELDS AT
THE READY

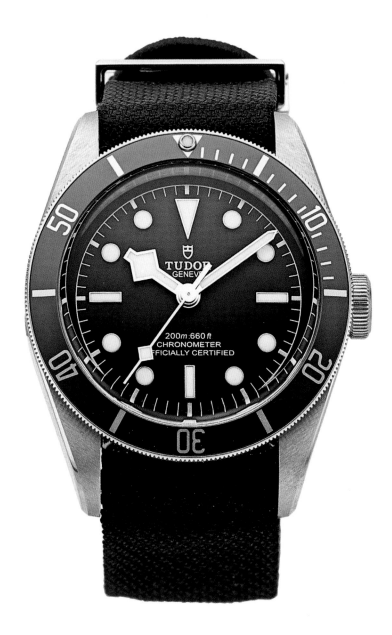

THE STORY OF TUDOR

It was once known – not in a complimentary way – as the "poor man's Rolex". It was marked by some as second-rate, as an also-ran – if only when compared to its big brother, Rolex.

Tudor, after all, may have been named to give a nod to the Rolex company's English roots, but it was created by Hans Wilsdorf quite deliberately as a cheaper alternative though not entirely a lesser one – for "when your aspirations run bigger than your bank balance", as the advertisement said. It had been an idea long in fruition too; Wilsdorf first registered the Tudor name back in 1926.

"For some years now I have been considering the idea of making a watch that our agents could sell at a more modest price than our Rolex watches, and yet one that could attain the standards of dependability for which Rolex is famous," he stated in an advertisement that marked the official launch of Tudor

OPPOSITE Tudor's Black Bay model, arguably the reborn brand's most cultish watch.

OPPOSITE Like
Rolex, Tudor too
experimented with
Quartz movements
through the 1980s,
as with this Prince
Quartz Oysterdate.

in 1946, and which, unusually, sought to explain the thinking behind the move. "I decided to form a separate company, with the object of making and marketing this new watch. And the instructions I gave – that it must be the best possible watch that could be made to sell at a medium price – have been magnificently carried out."

The creation of the Tudor Watch Company was a smart business decision too. By the mid-1940s, Rolex's reputation as a provider of durable, reliable, technologically advanced watches was assured. This was an opportunity to capitalize on that reputation with what would later be called a sub-brand or line extension. Here was an opportunity that would not be available to watchmakers without Rolex's established credentials.

By 1946 Rolex had already been quietly testing the reception to the Tudor name in the Australian market for 14 years, with some rare pieces stating both "Tudor" and "Rolex" on the dial. But then the association with Rolex was never hidden. Even the earliest Tudor watches offered Rolex's most distinctive and exclusive attributes – the airtight, dustproof and waterproof Oyster construction and the self-winding Perpetual movement. And they carried the Oyster name. They were also assembled in Rolex factories using many Rolex components. As collectors have concluded, these were virtually Rolex watches with another badge. Later Tudors would use off-the-shelf movement by specialist movement manufacturer ETA – the key differential from their Rolex equivalents.

Did that matter? If a Rolex watch, as tough as it was, might be considered refined by comparison, from the outset the company presented a Tudor watch as an everyday, all-action, reliable piece of equipment, to which Hans Wilsdorf publicly gave his personal endorsement.

The brand's shield logo – which went in and out of use over

Tudor's history — was entirely apt. In 1952 26 Tudor Oyster Princes were worn by members of the Royal Navy's year-long British scientific expedition to Greenland. The same year an advertisement wrote of its "Trial of Destruction", in which six Tudor watches were worn, one after the other, by a workman operating a pneumatic drill, meaning that each watch underwent "over one million tremendous shocks as the drill battered on granite rubble". It was, the ad claimed, "the hardest test watches have ever been put to". You guessed it: although "jarred beyond belief", all of the watches emerged in perfect functioning order.

This was just the first of a number of entertaining, if not exactly scientific, tests of the sturdiness of Tudor watches, as though to prove that cheaper did not mean weaker. One watch was worn by a stonecutter for three months, another by a coal miner for 252 hours while hacking away with a pick. A riveter of metal girders wore a Tudor, as did a motorcycle racer.

Yet behind every Tudor watch there was always the shadow of Rolex. Or, perhaps, with every Rolex would come an echo called Tudor. One of Tudor's more successful models was, inevitably, its own take on the Submariner, the ref 7900 series launched in 1954, just a year after the Rolex model of the same name — the case, bracelet and crown were all signed by Rolex, although Tudor would not refer to it as a Submariner until a new variant was launched in 1955. Many variations were produced almost straight away for the US Navy and France's Marine Nationale — a relationship that would last for the next two decades. For added panache the French Navy's divers refashioned old elastic parachute belts to make their own straps for their Submariners.

Tudor would also come to launch the kind of product more suited to office than offshore drilling — 1957 brought the Tudor Advisor, the only time it has produced a watch with a mechanical alarm function, and in 1970 came the Tudor

OPPOSITE Tudor allowed Rolex to be somewhat more adventurous in its use of colour, as with this 1970s grey/orange "Montecarlo" Oysterdate chronograph.

Oysterdate Chronograph – but its character remained rooted in robustness. It wasn't until 1969 that Tudor introduced a design detail for its Submariner which would finally set the entire brand apart from its elder sibling: out went Rolex Mercedes hands and in came a jagged hour hand dubbed the "snowflake".

Tudor would be remarkably open about its market position as a more affordable alternative. One print advertisement of the 1970s put it this way: "You might really want a Rolex GMT Master II, but let's be honest… Unless you spend $20k on jewellery for your wife, or buy a few two-tone Datejusts, there's no way you're ever getting that watch at MSRP from an authorised dealer. A Tudor GMT is an extremely capable alternative…"

But maybe the Rolex name – and its draw – was simply too big – and through the late 1970s and 1980s, increasingly reliant on the use of those ETA movements, the Tudor brand just faded away in many markets. Meanwhile, Rolex – having survived the watch industry's quartz crisis – went stratospheric.

The Tudor brand underwent a radical revival process from 2007 onward – including establishing itself as timing partner for the likes of Porsche and Ducati – but this time successfully shook off any lingering sense that it was in some way just a lesser Rolex. While 2012's Black Bay model, for one, quickly became something of a cult object, Tudor wisely underpinned these newly stylish watches – updates of forgotten designs pulled from the archives, an idea Rolex has historically been reluctant to pursue – with technical clout: the Black Shield model, of 2013, came with a single-piece ceramic case made entirely in-house, and Tudor's own in-house movement. In a sense, as Rolex became a luxury brand at luxury prices, Tudor filled the role that Rolex originally had so many decades before.

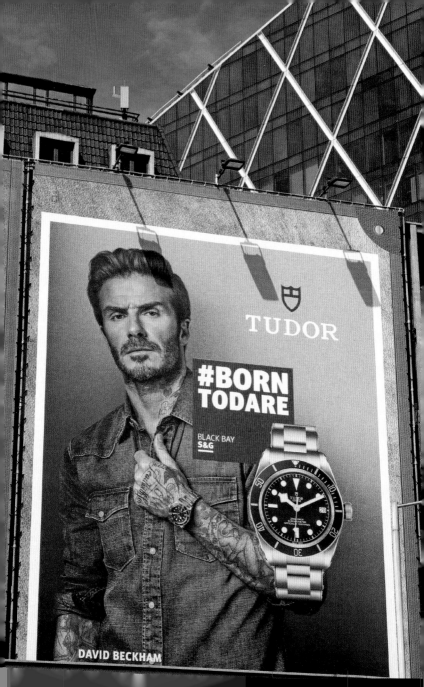

BIG-SCREEN
ACTION

ROLEX IN POPULAR CULTURE

The James Bond of the big screen might have worn an Omega watch since 1995, but before that he wore a Rolex. This was in keeping with the Bond of Ian Fleming's books.

I t was in *On Her Majesty's Secret Service* that Bond is described as wearing "a heavy Rolex Oyster Perpetual on a metal watch bracelet". In *Casino Royale* Fleming – who himself wore an Oyster Perpetual Explorer – was even more explicit: "He could not just wear a watch. It had to be a Rolex," he wrote of 007.

When the character made his cinematic debut, in 1962's *Dr. No*, Sean Connery wore a Rolex Submariner. By the third film of the series, Bond was sporting his Submariner on a nylon strap in the coloured stripes of the Royal Scots. Not only would the strap go on to be known as the Bond strap, but Rolex enthusiasts would come to refer to that exact model of watch – reference number 6538 – as the James Bond Submariner.

OPPOSITE Honor Blackman as Pussy Galore in *Goldfinger*, wearing a GMT-Master, one of the first cinematic examples of (the then novel idea of) a woman wearing a man's watch.

BELOW Vanessa
Redgrave in cult
1966 Antonioni film
Blow-Up, wearing a
Rolex Submariner.

Goldfinger also saw Pussy Galore, played by Honor Blackman, wear a Rolex GMT-Master – an early, perhaps the first, example of a woman in the public eye wearing a "man's watch". She was echoed in real life by the aviator Sheila Scott, the first person to fly over the North Pole in a light aircraft, among other achievements, and who subsequently appeared in a 1960 advertisement for, yes, the GMT-Master.

This association between secret agent and watch brand was one that only deepened over time: in the film version of *On Her Majesty's Secret Service*, Bond is seen wearing two Rolexes at different times, a Submariner 5513 and a Rolex Chronograph 6238 – a forerunner of the Daytona.

The watches, of course, would also come to have those special extras – the gadgets that so often helped Bond escape a tricky situation: in *Thunderball,* his Submariner has a built-in Geiger

BELOW Vanessa Redgrave in cult 1966 Antonioni film *Blow-Up,* wearing a Rolex Submariner.

counter; in *Live and Let Die,* the bezel rotates at speed to provide a useful buzz saw, while the watch can be highly magnetized such that it can even alter the path of a bullet – or unzip the back of a woman's dress. In the real world such a system would ruin the movements and result in some dreadful timekeeping.

The relationship on screen may not have lasted – Bond would go on to wear Seiko, TAG Heuer and a Rolex again, in *A Licence to Kill* – before Omega, now operating in the big business world of product placement, claimed that valuable real estate on Bond's wrist.

But Bond was just the most famous of Rolex's cinematic outings, many of them in what would become cult films: Robert de Niro in *The Deer Hunter*, Faye Dunaway in *Network*, Jennifer Connelly in *Top Gun: Maverick*, Gabriel Byrne in *The Usual Suspects* and Vanessa Redgrave in *Blow-Up* (she wore hers over her shirt cuff, as the Fiat industrialist and style icon Gianni

ABOVE The Daytona was long associated with Paul Newman when this model was awarded to the actor in 1995 after winning the 24 Hours of Daytona Race.

Agnelli made famous). There's also Michael Caine in a Datejust in *Get Carter* and Robert Shaw in a Submariner in *Jaws* – and these are just a few of the many films in which the star has a horological one to match, in the shape of a Rolex.

That the brand has become something of a go-to choice for costume designers – without any official marketing deal with the watchmaker – is arguably best explained by the simple fact that Rolex models are most established in their ability to project certain ideas about their character who wears them: usually something to do with being comfortably off, rather masculine and, typically, something of a winner.

Sometimes actors got to echo their own taste in watches for the character they played. On screen, Steve McQueen is perhaps more closely associated with TAG Heuer's Monaco watch. But off-screen, McQueen – like Paul Newman, whose character in *The Color of Money* explains he wears a Rolex because "it's the best" – was a huge Rolex fan. *The Hunter* was the only film in which McQueen got to wear his watch of choice, a Submariner. He got it just in time: the film would prove to be the actor's last.

The relationship between actor and watch brand would play out at auction in subsequent years. In 2017 a "Paul Newman" Daytona – the Rolex watch so called after the man with which it would come to be most closely associated – sold for US$ 17.75m, making it the most expensive wristwatch ever sold. But then this was the motherlode: the Paul Newman Daytona that had actually been owned by the actor himself. Two years later the Rolex GMT-Master worn by Marlon Brando in *Apocalypse Now* sold for just shy of US$ 2m all-in – and that's despite it missing the bezel. The actor had prised it off during filming to disguise the nature of the watch after refusing the director's request not to wear the potentially distracting model at all.

Such is the symbolic power of Rolex – a stand-in for wealth, a certain status and taste – that its role has gone beyond that

OPPOSITE
Inevitably the power of Rolex as a status symbol has made it a favourite of rap culture, and rap stars like a gold-laden Jay-Z.

RIGHT Tom Selleck as the star of *Magnum, P.I.* (1980-88), in his trusty Detroit cap and GMT watch.

of costume. "You see this watch? That watch costs more than your car," boasts the aggressive head honcho salesman in the 1992 film, *Glengarry Glen Ross*, pointing to his 18-carat gold Day-Date. For similar reasons of power play, Christian Bale appears to wear a Datejust as the monstrous Patrick Bateman in *American Psycho*. Actually he wears a Datejust lookalike by Seiko – because the filmmakers didn't want to offend Rolex by attaching the brand to a serial killer. The line "Don't touch the Rolex" from Bret Easton Ellis's novel – in which Rolex is namechecked 26 times – was likewise replaced in the film script with "Don't touch the watch". That experience did not stop Bale wearing Rolex for subsequent characters in *American Hustle* or *Vice*.

Small wonder too that Rolex would, by the mid-2010s, go on to become the "Exclusive Watch of the Academy of Motion Picture Arts and Sciences" and a sponsor of the Oscars.

As in films, so too in music. Bond may be a long way from dropping beats, but again, Rolex's status signalling and cultural cachet has inevitably made it a staple of rap lyrics. Rolex – or "Rollies" – may not be alone among luxury brands in being name-checked in rap, given its enthusiastic braggadocio. But few brands can claim mentions as numerous.

LEFT Sean Connery in a publicity photo for his role as James Bond, wearing – as Ian Fleming's creation did in the books – a Rolex.

WHAT'S IN A NAME?

Vital Seconds

OLD BOND STREET HOUSE,
6-8, OLD BOND STREET,
LONDON, W.1.

Dear Sirs,

I have now been using my Rolex Watch for some little while, and it is keeping perfect time under somewhat strenuous conditions.

I would like to congratulate you on having produced a very first-class Watch suitable for really rough treatment.

I was wearing it on the occasion of the J.C.C. Double 12 Hours Race on Friday and Saturday last, and the vibration which this Watch had to withstand during this long period has not upset its time-keeping properties in the least.

Yours faithfully,

M Campbell

Patent Nos. 260554, 274539, 281515.

THE WORLD-FAMOUS ROLEX MOVE-MENT SEALED AGAINST THE ELEMENTS

as worn by

SIR MALCOLM CAMPBELL

SIZES FOR MEN AND WOMEN:

Snowite . . £7 . 7 . 0
9 Carat . . £12 . 12 . 0
18 Carat . . £18 . 18 . 0
Luminous Dial 5/- extra.

Stocked by leading Jewellers throughout the British Empire. If any difficulty in obtaining, write to the Rolex Watch Co., Ltd., 40/44 Holborn Viaduct, E.C.1, for NAME OF NEAREST AGENT and a copy of our Golden Booklet containing beautiful illustrations of Rolex Watches.

Sole Agents for India :
J. Boseck & Co., Ltd., Calcutta and Darjeeling.
Lund & Blockley, Bombay.
P. Orr & Sons, Ltd., Madras and Rangoon.
Coombes & Co., Ltd., 118-122 Phayre Street, Rangoon.
Cooke & Kelvey, Calcutta, Delhi, Simla and Lahore.

NOTHING less than absolute precision can satisfy men who set out to create records, and for them the Rolex 'OYSTER' Wrist Watch, itself a holder of 25 World's Records, definitely has no equal.

The Rolex 'OYSTER' Wrist Watch is designed and assembled with quite as much care, with all the technical skill and attention as is devoted to the production of a giant racing-car. It is tested again and again, under the most exacting conditions, its performance over long periods is recorded and checked—it even passes through ovens and refrigerators and spends part of its time actually under water. Not until it emerges successfully through these adventures is it permitted to leave the works at Geneva.

Sir Malcolm Campbell himself wears a Rolex 'OYSTER,' and has been kind enough to give us his considered opinion of the watch, whilst refusing even the fee to which he as an expert would be entitled. We have his permission to publish his letter, and take this opportunity of thanking him for the trouble he has taken on our behalf.

THE ROLEX 'OYSTER' IS WATERPROOF AND SANDPROOF.

Insist on the genuine 'OYSTER' with the name Rolex on dial and movement. Resolutely and firmly refuse substitutes to avoid disappointment.

THE ROLEX
'OYSTER'
WRIST WATCH

THE ROLEX WATCH CO., LTD. (H. Wilsdorf, Managing Director), GENEVA & LONDON

THE MARKETING
OF ROLEX

While developing an association with the long-distance swimmer
and athlete Mercedes Gleitze was an innovation for the time,
Hans Wilsdorf soon recognized the potential of using celebrity
to sell Rolex watches.

In 1928 Wilsdorf signed up British actress Evelyn Laye,
whose name may have since been lost to history but who
was considered a remarkable beauty in her day. Or, as the
ads had it, she was the "famous and all-captivating" Evelyn Laye.
Consequently, Rolex's first two ambassadors, official or otherwise,
were both women.

That was not all that surprising – for all that Rolex was
more widely considered to be a manufacturer of watches for
men, albeit ones with a strong unisex appeal, the company
aimed equally at both sexes. In 1930 Rolex was advertising
itself to women as "leaders of fashion and precision", as a

OPPOSITE The first association for Rolex with a sportsperson was
with British racing driver Malcolm Campbell, best known for his world
speed records on both land and water.

ABOVE The Explorer II – the choice of skier Jean-Claude Killy – may not have matched the first Explorer for cult status, but arguably its standout orange hand made it more distinctive.

maker of objects that "please because of [their] beauty" as well as their usefulness. By the 1940s a Rolex was "for women in service", and by the 1950s models like the Princesse came with interchangeable straps to match your watch to your outfit. And a Rolex wasn't just for the kind of woman who regularly wore diamonds and ballgowns – "smart women, career-wise and socially conscious" would also do well to wear a Rolex, the company suggested, maybe one "fashioned after the famous men's Rolex Oyster".

Certainly Rolex would be mindful of the changing role of women in postwar Western society. The Haute Couture

Collection, "the watch for the bright new fashions", may have been aimed at women whose chief asset was their style or beauty, but by the 1960s Rolex was at least matching the idea that a watch could be pretty with the idea that it might be ideal for "the woman who is more than just a decoration", as one ad suggested in 1967. Hence the association with the likes of Sheila Scott, the first woman to fly solo around the world; she wore a GMT-Master.

Of course, Rolex didn't leave fashion behind entirely: it associated itself with Pucci and Ungaro, with avant-garde designer Rudi Gernreich – creator of the first thong swimwear and the topless monokini – and with British model Twiggy. And it wasn't above the sexism of the times: one ad features the racing driver Jackie Stewart with his wife, Helen. "Why Mr. Jackie Stewart wears a Rolex… [because] he appreciates the skills and care and patience that go into a piece of fine machinery, larger or small," the ad reads. "Why Mrs. Jackie Stewart wears a Rolex. Helen Stewart wears a Rolex because her husband gave her one." But this was also the moment when Rolex began really pushing to associate itself with excellence in performance and the figures of historic import behind this excellence.

That idea had always been there in the background. It was Malcolm Campbell who would become the first male ambassador of Rolex, during his attempts to break the land speed record. He would send a cablegram to Rolex noting that his "watch is still keeping perfect time – I was wearing it yesterday when Bluebird [his car] exceeded 3000mph [4800km/h]". Rolex subsequently used the cablegram in an advertisement, pointing out the Oyster's "27 world records for accuracy". And in an era when consumers were already growing doubtful of celebrities being paid to praise brands with which they were associated, the company added that it was thankful

Severiano Ballesteros takes the rough with the smooth. Just like his Rolex.

It seems odd that the ambition of one of the greatest golfers in the world, is to be a better golfer.

Seve Ballesteros, the youngest-ever winner of the British Open this century; the youngest-ever winner of the American Masters; and winner of countless international tournaments, has time on his side, however.

He thinks of nothing but golf. In every tournament, he thinks of nothing but the course.

And on every course, he thinks of nothing but the hole. "If I lose concentration, I lose the hole."

Since Seve was nine years old, practising clandestine golf strokes after hours on his home Pedrena golf course, sheer mental stamina has driven him to the top.

And enormous physical strength is what drives him out of the rough whenever his swash-buckling approach to the game takes him there.

Before a recent American tournament, he announced that he would try for eagles – two under par – at every hole. When advised that this would mean a lot of sixes and sevens, he replied "Sure . . . but many threes and they are very nice."

It is obviously no coincidence that Seve Ballesteros wears a watch which matches perfectly his precision-like personality and his never-ending quest for superiority. A Rolex Oyster Day-Date. Self-winding with day and date display.

"It's a very strong watch," he says. "Very, very tough. No water or sand can get in at all. I may have good days and bad days but this watch only has good days. And you know what? Every time I take a swing I'm winding it up.

"It's the perfect watch for me."

The unpredictable Ballesteros. And his entirely predictable Rolex. **ROLEX**
of Geneva

OPPOSITE Rolex has always been careful to associate itself with more "middle-class" sports and their champions – here, Seve Ballesteros, the winner of 90 professional golf titles.

LEFT Champion golfer Jack Nicklaus – in a gold Day-Date – raises the Claret Jug after winning the 1978 Open Championship. Sponsored sportspeople are careful to have their watch on show for the cameras.

for Campbell's message "more especially as he rejects the fee to which as an expert he is entitled for giving his opinion".

Campbell and Gleitz had both made headlines when Rolex capitalized on their fame, much as it would later associate itself with historic events like the attempts to scale Everest. But in 1967 – seven years after Hans Wilsdorf's death and going into a new era – the company made a more deliberate move into the world of sport, starting a partnership with championship golfer Arnold Palmer, and later with Gary Player and Jack Nicklaus – "the big three" of golf at that time.

This would become a key approach in its relationship with sports stars over the following decades. It aimed straight for the top, sponsoring not just the best players – when Tiger Woods won his first Masters victory in 14 years in 2019, he lifted the trophy wearing Rolex Deepsea – but also the globally televised major tournaments themselves, becoming an official partner and timekeeper.

It also associated itself with tennis, becoming official timekeeper for Wimbledon in 1978. The sight of the Rolex clock on Wimbledon's Centre Court is unmissable, making it irrelevant that most spectators are unlikely to buy the kind of Rolex worn by tennis legends such as Chris Evert or, later, Roger Federer – probably the most famous of players with which Rolex has been associated. Such is the association that the Datejust – historically awarded to Wimbledon winners – was made available in what came to be known as the Wimbledon dial, in slate grey with Roman numerals, like the clock.

Yet while Rolex spread its presence in sport far and wide, it was very careful about the sporting associations it made – and that meant sports more readily associated with high wealth and, yes, class. This meant not just golf and tennis, but figure skating and skiing, yachting, motorsport – including the 24 Hours of Le Mans and Rolex's own race at Daytona – and equestrianism – most notably both the Burghley and Badminton Horse Trials and the FEI World Equestrian Games. Its relationship with the arts is likewise skewed toward those more upscale and "intellectual" – including jazz and classical music, independent cinema and architecture.

Naturally, Rolex's sales and status were only boosted by the famous choosing to wear Rolex. Given the brand power of Rolex and – quite aside from their design or technical merit – the social symbolism of its watches, the list of celebrities who have worn this totem of success is seemingly endless. Better still, some are vocal in their passion for Rolex – among many others, Mark

OPPOSITE Rolex ran a long series of advertisements connecting extraordinary – and often rather macho – accomplishments with the likelihood of wearing one of its watches.

If you were flying the Concorde tomorrow

you'd wear a Rolex.

One essential piece of equipment in Pan Am's Concordes weighs nearly a quarter of a pound.

Which may seem a bit heavy for a watch.

But its Oyster case is carved from a solid block of hardened Swedish stainless steel (carved from 18 ct. gold it weighs even more). Inside its solid walls is a rotor self-winding officially certified chronometer. And outside, its big honest face tells the time in two time zones at once. And the date.

So much of the work is done by hand, it takes us more than a year to build a Rolex.

However, the Pan Am pilots who will fly the Concorde are rigorously demanding about the performance of their watch.

So if a Rolex weren't so heavy . . . it wouldn't fly.

The Rolex Pan Am pilots wear is the GMT-Master.

ROLEX
OF GENEVA

PAN AM Rolex — Official Timepiece Pan American World Airways.

Write to Rolex, Geneva, Switzerland, for free colour catalogue.

We invented the Submariner to work perfectly 660 feet under the sea.

It seems to work pretty well at any level.

The Rolex Submariner is a salty watch. It's the official watch for divers of the Royal Navy. That beefed-up Oyster case resists pressures down to 660 feet. You'll find it in the cockpits of most ocean racers as hard-driving skippers beat down to Bermuda, Hobart and the Fastnet Rock. How come it's seen so much where the wettest thing around is a dry Martini? Who knows. Maybe it's because the black dial goes so well with a black tie. Ask her. Maybe she knows.

ROLEX

When a man has a world in his hands, you expect to find a Rolex on his wrist

THE ROLEX WATCH COMPANY LIMITED *(founder: H. Wilsdorf)*, GENEVA, SWITZERLAND and in LONDON at 1 GREEN STREET, W.1

Wahlberg, Robert Downey Jr., Jason Statham, John Mayer, Eric Clapton, Lindsay Lohan and Ellen DeGeneres. That has made for the kind of profile, and credibility, that money cannot buy.

Auction houses have been quick to understand this when it comes to selling a Rolex too. Sure, Paul Newman did wear a Daytona, several variants of the Daytona mode, in fact – such that every Daytona tends to be spoken of with reference to the actor. Yet "Paul Newman Daytona" refers to specific "exotic dial" configurations, comprising contrasting colour minute track rings, Art Deco-style numbering on the black-on-white sub-dials and truncated hour markers.

LEFT In the late 1960s, Rolex unofficially sponsored Sheila Scott on her solo round-the-world and other long-distance flights – she was one of the first female public figures to wear a man's watch, the GMT-Master.

OPPOSITE Rolex was always alive not just to the utility of its watches, but also their appeal as status objects – even, perhaps, objects of seduction, as with this 1965 ad.

Likewise, those wishing to inflate the value of their lot often refer to the "Steve McQueen Explorer" (referencing the Explorer II) even though McQueen is not known to have ever worn the model – despite being a Rolex fan and a devotee of the Submariner. The Rolex Triple-Date Chronograph is likewise incorrectly connected to the Olympic skiing star Jean-Claude Killy – though he did actually wear the Explorer II and in the late 1960s starred in a "Peaks of Performance" ad campaign for Rolex doing so.

But then, as they say, celebrity sells – and for a company like Rolex that has always been true.

OPPOSITE A Rolex ambassador since 2006 – and arguably the brand's best of the modern era – the tennis legend Roger Federer, here wearing a Sky-Dweller, the most recent original Rolex model (at time of writing).

LEFT Rolex has rarely lacked for celebrity support in its bid to make its watches appeal as much to women as men. Here, Sophia Loren poses with hers in 1979.

A TIME
OF WAR

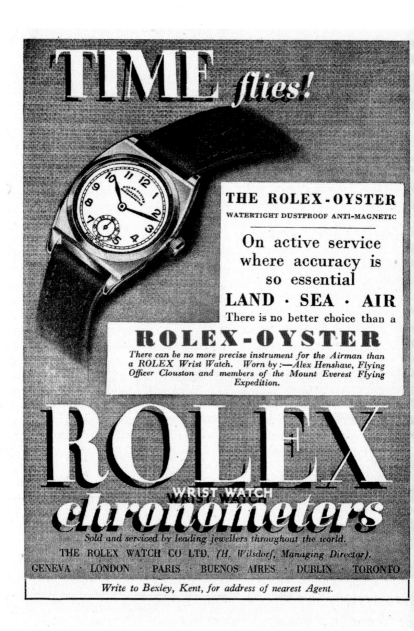

ROLEX AND
THE MILITARY

Although a German native, Rolex founder Hans Wilsdorf rejected
everything the Nazis stood for – so much so, in fact, that while
most watchmakers in neutral Switzerland profited from the
Second World War by supplying both sides of the conflict,
he chose to supply only the Allies.

R olex was also, after all, founded in the UK and
Wilsdorf's business partner was British. The company
would continue to use British-made parts in its watches
well into the 1950s.

Certainly the acclaimed toughness of Rolex's watches – a
characteristic on which the brand's reputation was built before it
came to be viewed as a status symbol – had by wartime already
been proven through various high-profile tests, among them
the first flight over Mount Everest in 1933 – the crew wearing
Rolexes – and Malcolm Campbell's attempts to break the land
speed record on Bonneville Flats in Utah in 1935. "Nothing less

OPPOSITE Rolex would use its supply to the servicemen of the Second
World War as a means of promoting the efficiency and durability of its
watches once the war ended.

ABOVE The
chronograph sold
in 1943 to British
Army Corporal Clive
James Nutting while
a prisoner of war,
and allegedly used
in the breakout
dramatized in
1963's war-drama
The Great Escape.

than absolute precision can satisfy men out to create records," as
an advertisement of the time suggested, adding – with a straight
face – that the Oyster Campbell wore was also "sandproof".

That helped give Rolexes appeal to anyone in the military.
Indeed, arguably it was Rolex's transformation of the wristwatch
– changing it from dainty accessory to hardy tool – that, from
the 1930s on, reimagined it as something a soldier, sailor or
airman might feasibly wear. And on occasion trust with his life.
Chuck Yeager, the first pilot to fly faster than the speed of sound,
bought a Rolex Oyster Perpetual for himself and wore it on his
numerous test flights. After his record-breaking flight in 1947,
he sent a signed photo to Rolex, complete with a little doodle
of the five-point crown.

It was the Italian watchmaker Panerai that looked to Rolex's
waterproof housing when it came to develop a diving watch
for the frogman commandos of the First Submarine Group
Command. The resulting watch, the first Radiomir – ref 3646

– may have been named for the luminescent material that made it so easy to read deep under water, but it worked because it had a Rolex Oyster case and movement. The two companies would work together on creating watches for the Italian military up until 1956 – with, of course, a gap in that history while Italy was allied to Germany during the Second World War.

The legibility of Rolex watches – with their clear and (for the time) large dials – made them a favourite of Royal Air Force pilots in the run-up to the war, many being bought privately by them. (Unfortunately, a Rolex was not yet a standard issue piece of military equipment.) This prefigured the off-the-books commissioning of Rolex to produce extremely limited editions of its models for special divisions of the armed forces for many decades that followed.

It was the RAF's success in defending the UK during the Battle of Britain in 1940 that inspired Wilsdorf to charge his team with the design of a series of high-visibility, three-handed

BELOW Rolex watches created for officers of the First World War invariably borrowed from pocket watches' cases to protect the glass from knocks.

"Air" models specifically for these aviators – the Air Lion, Air Tiger and the Air Giant. Production of these models ceased by the end of the war in 1945, with the exception of one model that has been in almost continuous production since its introduction in 1945, the Air-King.

Later, when associating the watch with wartime seemed less appropriate, the Cold War provided some kind of context for the appeal of the Air-King and its variants, including the Air-King Date. A 1963 advertisement in the *New Scientist* noted how "the man with the top-secret job wears a Rolex on his wrist" – unlike his watch, the job of the bespectacled, white lab-coated man at his oscillator is not precise, but it involves "all-important research".

But back to the Second World War: Wilsdorf also considered it a duty to get his watches to Allied servicemen wherever they might be – and, remarkably, thanks to a special service he organized, even Allied prisoners of war were able to order an Oyster by letter and direct from their prison camps. They were, of course, not in a position to pay. But Wilsdorf took a serviceman's word as his bond – or, at least, an officer's – and was happy to wait for payment after the war's end. This inevitably boosted morale since the arrangement implied that the Axis forces would not win.

And an Oyster proved very useful. Corporal Clive James Nutting was imprisoned at the German prison camp Stalag Luft III. There, he ordered an expensive 3525 chronograph – later dubbed the Monoblocco for having a one-piece construction – and, although only a non-commissioned officer, Wilsdorf afforded him the same "buy now, pay later" arrangement. Stalag Luft III would, in 1944, be the site of the one of the largest prison camp breakouts of the war, its story going on to be told in first the book, then the film *The Great Escape*. Nutting's watch was said to be used to time the best moment for prisoners to leave the tunnels and make a run for the cover of the nearby trees.

OPPOSITE The Air-King is the only surviving production model of a series of watches launched soon after the Second World War and inspired by the actions of the RAF.

Perhaps as a means of acknowledging how Britain's wartime leader had led the country to victory, Winston Churchill was selected to receive the 100,000th certified chronometer produced by Rolex – an 18-carat gold Rolex Oyster Perpetual Datejust.

It would not be until after the war, however, that official military watches by Rolex would come into service, the first being in the United States. That was in 1953, when the US Air Force's acrobatic team, the Thunderbirds, adopted Rolex's Turn-O-Graph model – its first with a rotating bezel, so useful in recording elapsed time, and also the first in the two-tone Rolesor gold and steel combination. Indeed, it was effectively only this elite group of flyers that can be said to have fully embraced the model, because while it remained in the Rolex collection for more than 50 years, it never quite proved to be a commercial success and was finally discontinued in 2011.

But the British Ministry of Defence was right behind the Thunderbirds: in 1954 it selected the ref 6528 "big crown"

RIGHT Arguably the Holy Grail of vintage Rolexes, the MilSub Submariner was made in limited numbers to a particular military specification.

Rolex Submariner to undergo tests with a view to it becoming standard issue for the Royal Navy and, most obviously, for its submariners. Rolex sent some 50 examples of the watch and the Navy, happy with its performance in the field, adopted it as standard issue in 1957. This model, of course, is better known as the James Bond Submariner. And, since Ian Fleming – who served in Naval Intelligence during the Second World War – decided to give his character the rank of Commander in the Royal Navy, Sean Connery also wore a Submariner in *Dr. No*, released five years later.

The Submariner would also become the watch of choice of the US Navy's elite Navy SEALs and of its submariners too – "If you shipped out on the *Skate*, the *Shark* or the *Nautilus* [all US submarines], you'd recognise this face," as one ad had it, the face referring to that of the Submariner watch.

OPPOSITE The
more obscure Turn-
O-Graph model,
with a rotating
Thunderbird bezel
which, like dive
watches, allows
the recording of
elapsed time.

The MilSub or military edition of the Submariner would become arguably the most collectible of all Rolexes – in part because not many were made and few survived to enter the secondary market, in part because of the military provenance, and in part because they would come to be regarded as Rolex's ultimate expression of the no-nonsense tool watch, thanks to a number of design tweaks that made it differ from the civilian model.

Spring bars – the metal rods onto which a strap is attached to the watch, mounted on small springs for easy removal – were replaced by solid bars soldered into place; the bezel was made from nickel silver (actually a silver-free copper alloy) rather than brass, so it could dent if bashed but would not break; and it was also made slightly larger, so that it extended beyond the edge of the case, making it easier to grab when wearing gloves. On the even rarer models later issued to the British Special Forces – about 1,200 pieces were issued to the Special Boat Service and the Special Air Service – the steel and aluminium bezel showed markings for the full 60 minutes (instead of just the first 15), the Mercedes hands were replaced with Sword hands, and a telltale T in a white circle on the dial indicated the use of tritium for the luminescence.

Three more iterations of the standard issue MilSub followed over the years to 1967 – taking on the Special Forces enhancements – when the James Bond parallel could be drawn again: the Royal Navy dropped the Submariner in favour of the Omega Seamaster 300. But this arrangement lasted for only four years, before they returned to the Submariner. Finally, in 1979 the Ministry of Defence unsurprisingly seems to have concluded that outfitting its seamen in a Rolex was just that bit too extravagant, given ever-tighter budgets. The contract with the watchmaker was, like many a Bond villain, terminated.

OLD TIMERS

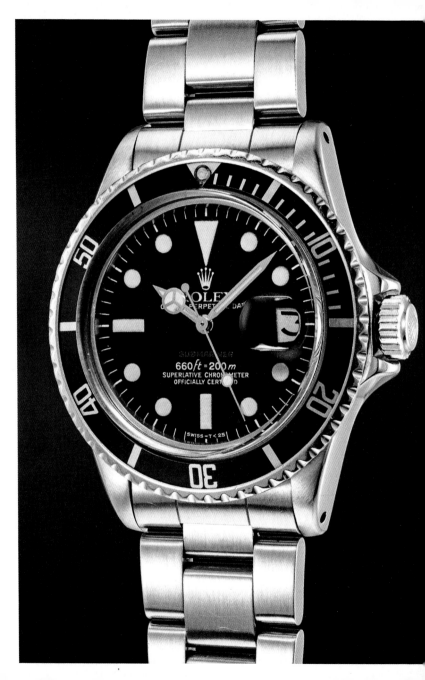

VINTAGE ROLEX

If you're wondering whether it's a good thing that the bezel on
the vintage watch you're considering is "ghosted", or whether
that means it's already dead, or whether "tropical" means a dial
is suitable only for jungle treks or Bali's beaches, or quite why
a "double red" is so much pricier than a mere "single red", then
welcome to the esoteric world of vintage Rolexes.

A secondary market for Rolex watches has slowly but
steadily grown since the 1980s – partly because buying
certain new Rolexes can prove such a challenge,
to the extent that some rare Rolex models are only available
"pre-worn"; partly because of Rolex's brand power and
desirability; and partly because they tend to hold their value.
Inevitably, where Rolex leads, the vintage Rolex market follows:
a new Submariner, for example, sparks interest in vintage
Submariners. And a spike in prices.

OPPOSITE A superb "single red" Submariner. Clear here is the effect
of the Cyclops date magnifier, said to be inspired by Hans Wilsdorf's
second wife's myopia.

Certainly Rolex has grown to dominate the vintage watch market at large. Indeed, the effects of ageing on a Rolex watch have come to be regarded by fans not as flaws but as highly desirable signs of collectible uniqueness. This was noted by David Silverman, of London-based The Vintage Watch Company – arguably the world's biggest dealer in vintage Rolexes at the time of writing – and has been demonstrated by prices at auction. By contrast, Rolex itself pushes the boundaries of engineering and materials science precisely to stop these effects of ageing. In the future, "vintage" Rolexes may look as good as the day they were made.

In the meantime, what used to be the insider language of a trade has, in no small way thanks to the internet and social media, become the unifying if geeky language of a community of watch fans – and especially fans of Rolex, the brand with which much of the lingo originated and to which it still most readily applies.

Now Rolex collectors talk of the small differences between very similar models which give them one-off combinations of dial, bezel and luminescent effects, shaped by that watch's years of exposure to sunlight, heat and moisture. To one man, such effects merely make a Rolex watch look old or tired. To the vintage Rolex fan, it makes that watch look special. Other collectors, meantime, express their regard for Rolex through affectionate nicknames for certain finishes, colour combinations or use of typography. Outsiders to the cult of Rolex may think this verges on madness – and all the more so when such details command a handsome premium.

FADED: Any Rolex with a paint-based dial will fade over time, though there needs to be a distinct shift from the original to count a watch as properly "faded". Dealers and collectors

will, however, sometimes refer to specific shades: for example, an originally red bezel may be described as faded to, specifically "fuchsia" – the Pantone shade that the bezel of a 1960s/70s Rolex GMT makes its way toward under certain conditions – or to "root beer", a light brown.

GHOST BEZEL: This references an even more specific fade on Rolex dive watch bezels that start out black and end up a distinctive shade of grey to pale grey – often at a cost to the legibility of the numerals and so the functionality of the watch. But it's an extremely rare effect of light and temperature and so can command bigger premiums. Other black bezels fade to shades of navy or brown, but the trade has yet to coin words for these.

ABOVE The GMT Master II, with its independent third hour hand and, with this 2018 example, the signature Pepsi bezel in ceramic.

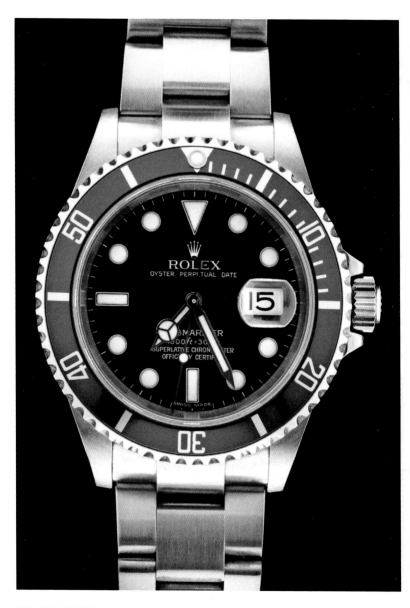

TROPICAL: This indicates a distinctive colour change that comes about only when a Rolex watch has been exposed to long periods of intense heat and wet – hence "tropical". Typically the change is from black to a golden brown and the effect is subtle, varying in different light. But it's sufficiently fascinating that there are collectors who focus their attention on one Rolex model/reference of watch, each instance of which looks distinct, thanks to their tropical dials.

PEPSI BEZEL: This typically refers to a Rolex sports model bezel in two contrasting shades of blue and red – very close to those used on the soft drink can. The name, of course, teams one global brand with another and, deliberately or not, underscores the contrast in their accessibility. At the time of writing Pepsi dials are still being made, unlike the Coke bezel – in black and red. Rolex collectors alike seem to enjoy creating off-beat colour references for watches – a Rolex diving watch with a dial or bezel in a familiar shade of green? That's a "Starbucks" model, of course, distinct from a "Hulk" or a "Kermit".

OPPOSITE Submariners with green bezels have affectionately been nicknamed the likes of "Kermit", "Hulk" or "Starbucks" by Rolex fans.

BELOW The world of vintage Rolex has its own language: here, a JPS or John Player Special black dial/yellow gold Daytona, so named for its cigarette brand-like colour combination.

DOUBLE RED: Rolex collectors can obsess over the smallest of differences which nonetheless signal the rarity of a particular model. Rolex's first Sea-Dweller model, for example, came with two lines of red text on the dial, as opposed to certain models of (now vintage) Submariner, which had only one – hence the former being dubbed the "double red", the latter "single red". Or, for that matter, the "big red" of lettering on certain models of Daytona. Other typographic details on vintage models can also add to their appeal for collators – for example, a small capital T in a circle, denoting a MilSub or military issue Submariner; or the presence of the COMEX logo on the dial, indicating a post-1970 Submariner, or later Sea-Dweller, made in very limited numbers for the French diving company, Compagnie Maritime D'Expertises, and never commercially released.

ROULETTE DATE: Love a splash of red on a Rolex dial? How about a "roulette" date display, more commonplace in the brand's watches of the 1940s and 1950s, and revised on the Datejust during the 1970s. A roulette date display is one that alternates between red and black: red for even days, black for odd ones.

PUMPKIN LUME: Ever wondered why watchmakers today sometimes give the luminescent material on the numerals and hands of their watch dials a certain warm sepia tone? That's to mimic the effects of age on lume – over time it turns a characterful shade of what the watch trade considers pumpkin-like. Many makers, Rolex included, would never design a new watch to look artificially old this way – but if its luminescence has faded to this distinctive tone, value is only added.

LEFT A Rolex GMT-Master showing all the signs of a life of action, most notably through its attractively discoloured "tropical" dial.

JPS: A term that may be long out of date, or culturally limited in its reach, but that doesn't stop the vintage Rolex watch market from continuing to use it. JPS describes a colour combination of black and gold, often in reference to a Rolex "Paul Newman" Daytona. Why "JPS"? That's a reference to John Player Specials, which sponsored a Formula One Lotus team through the 1970s, with the cars in its signature black and gold livery.

INDEX

CREDITS

The publishers would like to thank the following sources for their kind permission to reproduce the pictures in this book.